T0258783

Realistic Image Synthesis
Using Photon Mapping

Realistic Image Synthesis Using Photon Mapping

Henrik Wann Jensen

Department of Computer Science
Stanford University

CRC Press
Taylor & Francis Group
Boca Raton   London   New York

CRC Press is an imprint of the
Taylor & Francis Group, an **informa** business

AN A K PETERS BOOK

Editorial, Sales, and Customer Service Office

A K Peters, Ltd.
888 Worcester Street, Suite 230
Wellesley, MA 02482
www.akpeters.com

Library of Congress Cataloging-in-Publication Data

Jensen, Henrik Wann, 1969–
    Realistic image synthesis using photon mapping / Henrik Wann Jensen.
        p. cm.
    Includes bibliographic references and index.
    ISBN 1-56881-147-0 (hardcover)
    1. Computer graphics. I. Title.

T385 .J48 2001
006.6–dc21   2001033844

Printed in Canada
09 08 07 06 05   11 10 9 8 7 6 5 4 3 2

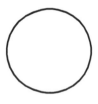

Foreword

Making realistic images using a computer is now commonplace. As a result, directors can create convincing, imaginary worlds; and designers can virtually prototype, visualize, and evaluate potential products and spaces. Although not that long ago it was easy for anyone to distinguish computer-generated images from photographs, nowadays even experts are easily fooled. It is hard to separate the real from the virtual in a movie or magazine these days.

However, creating algorithms and building systems to produce such images is a challenging task. Fundamentally it involves understanding the physics—how light interacts with the materials in the world—and the psychophysics—how we perceive the light rays entering our eye. Artists and scientists throughout the ages have studied the causes of appearance and the resulting visual cues: motion, shape, occlusion, perspective, lighting, reflection, texture, and color. All these generators of appearance may now be modeled on a computer. We can model and simulate the processes that form patterns and textures, the physics of light reflecting from a surface or scattering in a media, and the propagation of light as it travels from light sources through the scene to the camera.

The two breakthrough algorithms in image synthesis were ray tracing and radiosity. Ray tracing involves first casting rays from the eye through a pixel and into the scene, recursively generating reflected and refracted rays. Stochastic or distributed ray tracing was invented to deal with motion blur, depth of field and reflections from glossy surfaces, and path tracing extended the algorithm to deal with mutual interreflection. Radiosity takes a different approach: it assumes the world consists of diffuse surface patches, and then solves a matrix equation for the amount of light reaching each patch.

Over the past 15 years or so, these algorithms have been studied and refined. The common physics of light and light transport has been identified and unified into Kajiya's rendering equation. This equation is now expressed in precisely-defined physical quantities such as radiance and the bidirectional reflectance-distribution function. An applied mathematician recognizes the rendering equation as an integral equation. And a numerical analyst maps these different approaches onto the basic methods of scientific computing; path tracing is an example of the application of the Monte Carlo Method (the generalized algorithm we call Monte Carlo Ray Tracing or MCRT), and radiosity is an example of the application of the finite element method.

Time has also indicated that the most general and robust approach is Monte Carlo Ray Tracing. In order to apply finite element methods to image synthesis requires simplifying assumptions. For example, surfaces are assumed to be diffuse and planar; generalizing the finite element formulation for non-diffuse surfaces and complex geometries has proven to be practically and theoretically very difficult. Unfortunately, Monte Carlo Ray Tracing has also had its problems. Brute force application of the Monte Carlo Method to image synthesis leads to a very slow algorithm; as a result, not enough rays are traced and the resulting images often are noisy. This has limited the usability of MCRT in production environments.

But recently a breakthrough occurred: a subtle and simple method— Photon Mapping—was invented by Henrik Wann Jensen to speedup MCRT. The idea is to break ray tracing into two passes: the first casts photons into the scene from the light sources, and the second collects the photons to produce an image. Although this idea had been proposed and tried by others, to get good results meant it must be implemented with great care. This book describes how to do it right. It presents the entire story, from the theory of why it works to the practice of how to add it to your system.

Photon mapping means that indirect lighting may be computed efficiently and robustly. Now we can add a whole new class of scenes to the repertoire of computer-generated imagery. These include dazzling underwater pictures of streaming beams of light, outdoor illumination of clouds and landscapes, light focusing through a glass of cognac, and more recently translucent materials such as marble. Read the book, implement the algorithm, and enjoy the images!

Pat Hanrahan

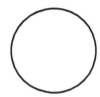

Contents

Preface   xv

1 Introduction   1
   1.1 Realistic Image Synthesis   2
   1.2 Global Illumination   3
        1.2.1 Ray-Tracing Techniques   4
        1.2.2 Finite Element Radiosity Techniques   5
        1.2.3 Hybrid and Multi-Pass Techniques   6
        1.2.4 Photon Mapping   7
   1.3 Overview of This Book   7

2 Fundamentals of Global Illumination   11
   2.1 The Nature of Light   11
   2.2 Lighting Terminology   13
        2.2.1 Radiometry   13
        2.2.2 Photometry   15
        2.2.3 The Solid Angle   16
   2.3 Light Emission   17

2.4   Light Scattering   18
   2.4.1   The BSSRDF   18
   2.4.2   The BRDF   19
   2.4.3   The Reflectance   20
   2.4.4   Diffuse Reflection   21
   2.4.5   Specular Reflection   22
   2.4.6   Reflection Models   24
2.5   The Rendering Equation   27
   2.5.1   The Radiosity Equation   29
   2.5.2   Neumann Series Expansion   29
   2.5.3   Path Integral Formulation   30
2.6   Light Transport Notation   30

3   Monte Carlo Ray Tracing   33
3.1   Classic Ray Tracing   34
   3.1.1   Algorithm   36
3.2   Path Tracing   37
   3.2.1   Algorithm   42
3.3   Bidirectional Path Tracing   43
   3.3.1   Algorithm   47
3.4   Metropolis Light Transport   47
   3.4.1   Algorithm   50

4   The Photon-Mapping Concept   51
4.1   Motivation   51
4.2   Developing the Model   53
4.3   Overview   54

5   Photon Tracing   55
5.1   Photon Emission   55
   5.1.1   Diffuse Point Light   56
   5.1.2   Spherical Light   57
   5.1.3   Square Light   58
   5.1.4   Directional Light   58
   5.1.5   Complex Light   58
   5.1.6   Multiple Lights   59
   5.1.7   Projection Maps   59
5.2   Photon Scattering   60
   5.2.1   Specular Reflection   60
   5.2.2   Diffuse Reflection   60
   5.2.3   Arbitrary BRDF Reflection   61
   5.2.4   Russian Roulette   61

5.3   Photon Storing   64

6   The Photon Map Data Structure   67
6.1   The Data Structure   67
6.2   Photon Representation   69
6.3   The Balanced Kd-Tree   70
      6.3.1   Memory Layout   71
      6.3.2   Balancing Algorithm   71
6.4   Locating the Nearest Photons Efficiently   72
      6.4.1   Algorithm   72

7   The Radiance Estimate   75
7.1   Density Estimation   75
7.2   Derivation   77
7.3   Algorithm   80
7.4   Filtering   80
      7.4.1   The Cone Filter   81
      7.4.2   The Gaussian Filter   82
      7.4.3   Differential Checking   83
7.5   Photon Gathering   83

8   Visualizing the Photon Map   85
8.1   Rendering Caustics   86
8.2   Rendering Color Bleeding   87
      8.2.1   Excluding Direct Illumination   89
8.3   Fast Approximations   89
8.4   Caustics Examples   91
      8.4.1   Reflection Inside a Ring   91
      8.4.2   Prism with Dispersion   91
      8.4.3   Caustics on a Non-Lambertian Surface   92
      8.4.4   A Glass of Cognac on a Rough Surface   92

9   A Practical Two-Pass Algorithm   95
9.1   Overview   95
9.2   Solving the Rendering Equation   96
9.3   Pass 1: Photon Tracing   97
      9.3.1   The Caustics Photon Map   97
      9.3.2   The Global Photon Map   99

9.4   Pass 2: Rendering 100
      9.4.1   Direct Illumination 101
      9.4.2   Specular and Glossy Reflection 102
      9.4.3   Caustics 102
      9.4.4   Multiple Diffuse Reflections 103
9.5   Examples 104
      9.5.1   The Four Rendering Components 105
      9.5.2   Fractal Box 105
      9.5.3   Box with Water 106
      9.5.4   Global Illumination on a Point Cloud 110
      9.5.5   A Mountain Landscape 110
      9.5.6   The Courtyard House by Mies van der Rohe 111

10 Participating Media   113
   10.1 Light Scattering in Participating Media 114
   10.2 The Volume Rendering Equation 115
   10.3 The Phase Function 115
         10.3.1 Isotropic Scattering 116
         10.3.2 The Henyey-Greenstein Phase Function 116
         10.3.3 The Schlick Phase Function 117
         10.3.4 Other Phase Functions 118
   10.4 Ray Marching 119
         10.4.1 Adaptive Ray Marching 121
   10.5 Photon Tracing 121
         10.5.1 Photon Scattering 123
         10.5.2 Photon Storing 123
         10.5.3 Photon Emission 123
   10.6 The Volume Radiance Estimate 124
   10.7 Rendering Participating Media 125
   10.8 Subsurface Scattering 127
         10.8.1 Photon Tracing 127
         10.8.2 Rendering 128
   10.9 Examples 129
         10.9.1 Rising Smoke 129
         10.9.2 Smoke Flowing past a Sphere 129
         10.9.3 A Volume Caustic 130
         10.9.4 Michelangelo's David 130
         10.9.5 A Weathered Granite Sphinx 134
         10.9.6 A Translucent Marble Bust 135

11 Optimization Strategies   139
  11.1 Irradiance Caching   139
      11.1.1 Irradiance Gradients   142
      11.1.2 Irradiance Caching and Photon Mapping   143
  11.2 Importance Sampling   144
  11.3 Visual Importance   145
      11.3.1 A Three-Pass Technique   147
  11.4 Efficient Stratification of Photons   147
  11.5 Faster Shadows with Shadow Photons   148
  11.6 Precomputed Irradiance   151
  11.7 Parallel Computations   151

A Basic Monte Carlo Integration   153
  A.1 The Sample Mean Method   153
  A.2 Variance-Reduction Techniques   154

B A Photon Map Implementation in C++   157

C A Cognac Glass Model   167

Bibliography   169

Index   181

Preface

This book is a practical as well as an in-depth guide to photon mapping. Photon mapping is an efficient global illumination technique for realistic image synthesis that has been developed in computer graphics in the last few years. The main advantages of photon mapping compared to other image synthesis techniques is that it is both very versatile and fast. With photon mapping it is easy to simulate caustics (for example, the light focused through a glass onto a table), color bleeding (such as the soft reddening of a white wall due to light reflected off an adjacent red carpet), participating media (for example, a room filled with smoke), and subsurface scattering (particularly noticeable in translucent materials such as marble, where light propagates into the material). Several illumination effects such as caustics on arbitrary surfaces, volume caustics, and general subsurface scattering were first simulated using photon mapping. In addition the method is very practical, and several commercial and free software rendering packages have started adding support for photon mapping.

Anyone with an interest in realistic image synthesis should find this book useful. Technical directors and others interested in rendering will find a description of what is under the hood in many rendering packages. Understanding this will make it much easier to control the rendering software. Experienced readers who have implemented a ray tracer should be able to take the information in this book and immediately begin simulating caustics as well as global illumination and participating media. To ease such an implementation, the appendix includes source code for the photon map data structure. Experts should also find the book useful as it gives the details of the photon mapping method and provides a much more coherent description than the existing papers.

My motivation for writing this book is a hope that more people will be able to enjoy the creation of photorealistic images as I have for many years. I developed the photon mapping algorithm as part of my PhD studies in 1993-1994 and published the first papers on the method in 1995-1996. The "photon map" name was introduced in 1994. After using the concept of illumination maps (texture maps with illumination) for some time, the idea of storing individual photons made the name photon map seem natural. Later, I discovered that this name is used in physics as well for a very similar concept (a map of photon hits). In 1998 and 1999 I was involved in the extension of the method to simulate participating media and subsurface scattering. You will find these extensions and much more explained in detail in this book.

At the ACM SIGGRAPH conference in 2000 I presented a course with Niels Jørgen Christensen entitled "A practical guide to global illumination using photon maps". This book significantly extends the material that was written for this course. The course notes included a substantial amount of material from my PhD dissertation—this book even more so. In addition several chapters with background information have been added and the description of the photon mapping algorithm has been extended significantly, including a new chapter on participating media and a new chapter on optimization strategies. The reference list has also been expanded to include more than 120 publications. This should make it easy for the interested reader to obtain more information. Finally, the book includes an implementation of the photon map that should be very easy to integrate in a ray-tracing program.

It is my hope that this book will serve both as a useful tutorial and as a reference book. It contains many rendered images as well as little notes, tips, and formulas that I have collected through the years, and that I wished could have been found in one place.

Acknowledgements

Thanks to Pat Hanrahan for providing me with a very stimulating environment at Stanford University, for letting me take the time to write this book, and for contributing the Foreword.

The seed for this book was the SIGGRAPH 2000 course on photon mapping. Thanks to Niels Jørgen Christensen for being involved in this course and to Per Henrik Christensen for being very supportive and contributing to the course material. Cheers to Alan Chalmers for suggesting this course in the first place over a beer in Key West.

Special thanks to Maryann Simmons and Steve Marschner for very detailed and insightful comments and for reviewing several drafts of this book. Also, many thanks to Philip Dutré, Eric Lafortune, Tim Purcell, Peter Shirley, and Frank Suykens for expert comments on most of the sections of the book.

Thanks to Ron Fedkiw for providing the smoke simulations used to illustrate participating media, and to Julie Dorsey for giving me permission to use the weathered models of the Sphinx and the marble bust model. Thanks to Marc Levoy for letting me use the model of Michelangelo's David, and to the graphics group at the University of Utah for allowing me use the model of Little Matterhorn. Thanks to Stephen Duck for modeling and letting me use Ludwig Mies "Courtyard House with Curved Elements."

Many thanks to A K Peters. To Alice and Klaus Peters for suggesting that I write this book, and to the staff at A K Peters (particularly Ariel Jaffee) for being instrumental in making this book a reality.

Finally, thanks to my family, friends, and colleagues for being very understanding of the time-consuming process it is to write a book.

Henrik Wann Jensen
May 2001

1

Introduction

The world around us contains many beautiful phenomena. In the outdoors we can experience amazing sunsets, moonlight scattered through clouds, early morning fog at a lake, underwater sunbeams, and much more as described by Minnaert in his classic book [66]. If we move inside we can see flames in the fireplace, light focused through a glass of cognac onto a table, the translucent appearance of an orchid, steam rising from a cup of coffee, the soft flickering illumination from a candle flame. The list is endless.

Today we can simulate these phenomena with computers. The creation of realistic-looking synthetic images has reached a state that makes it possible to simulate almost any phenomena. We can render images of sunsets and sunrises using computers without having to wait for a clear day and the right time. We cannot yet reproduce the same experience as being outside observing a sunset, but this is mainly a limitation of the display devices available, and not a limitation of the underlying global illumination algorithms.

The last few years have seen an explosion in the use of computer graphics and realistic image synthesis. This is particularly the case in the entertainment industry where movies often make extensive use of computer-

Figure 1.1. A wireframe rendering of a model (upper left) blended with a full global illumination simulation of sunlight entering the house (lower right).

generated special effects that seamlessly integrate with real filmed footage. Computer games are presenting increasingly realistic worlds in real time getting closer to the dream of virtual reality. Outside entertainment, synthetic photorealistic images are used in design, architecture, hospitals, education, advertising, and more. These areas also use non-photorealistic images (such as technical illustrations), but the "final product" is most often presented using photorealistic rendering. This is often the most natural visualization technique since it is what we are used to seeing.

1.1   Realistic Image Synthesis

Realistic image synthesis is the process of creating synthetic images that are indistinguishable from images (such as photographs) of the real world. Ever since the first lines and dots were generated using computers there has been substantial interest in the creation of synthetic photorealistic images. The first techniques for this purpose were naturally limited by the available

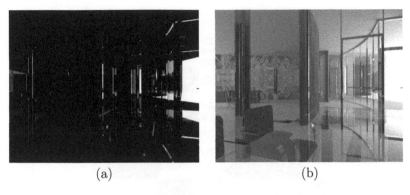

(a)   (b)

Figure 1.2. Global illumination algorithms simulate *all* light reflections in a scene. The images show a daylight simulation of an architectural model. Image (a) was rendered using ray tracing and contains only direct illumination and specular reflections while (b) was rendered using photon mapping and has global illumination. (See Color Plate III.)

technology and were mainly hacks to obtain a desired effect, such as smooth appearance and highlights. It was not until 1980 with the introduction of ray tracing and 1984 with the introduction of radiosity that realistic image synthesis began using physically-based simulations. These methods make extensive use of the physical nature of light, and they both existed in other fields prior to their introduction in computer graphics, with ray tracing being popular in optics and radiosity being widely used for problems in heat transfer.

1.2   Global Illumination

The physically-based simulation of all light scattering in a synthetic model is called global illumination. The goal of global illumination is to simulate all reflections of light in a model and enable an accurate prediction of the intensity of the light at any point in the model. The input to a global illumination simulation is a description of the geometry and the materials as well as the light sources. It is the job of the global illumination algorithm to compute how light leaving the light sources interacts with the scene. Figure 1.2 shows an example of an architectural model rendered with and without global illumination. There is a substantial visual difference between the two renderings. The global illumination simulation is necessary to capture the indirect illumination that is illuminating most of the model. These effects are critical for realistic image synthesis; without them the illumination often looks flat and synthetic.

Figure 1.3. A typical ray-traced image. Ray tracing is good at rendering mirror reflections, and spheres are very simple to ray trace.

Several global illumination algorithms have been developed. Most of them are based on two major techniques:

- Point sampling (ray tracing)

- Finite elements (radiosity)

In addition, there are hybrid techniques combining both radiosity and ray tracing. Each of these methods has strengths and weaknesses, and the following sections contain a brief review of these methods.

1.2.1   Ray-Tracing Techniques

Ray tracing is a point-sampling technique that traces infinitesimal beams of light through a model. Basic ray tracing as introduced in 1980 [120] traces light rays backwards from the observer to the light sources. This approach can only handle mirror reflections/refractions and direct illumination. Important effects such as depth of field, motion blur, caustics, indirect illumination, and glossy reflection cannot be computed. To simulate these effects ray tracing has been extended with Monte Carlo methods [21, 20, 52] in which rays are distributed stochastically to account for all light paths. Monte Carlo ray-tracing methods can simulate all types of light scattering. The only problem these methods have is variance—seen as noise in the rendered images. Eliminating this noise requires a large number of sample rays. Several researchers have investigated how to reduce the noise by distributing rays more carefully [41, 58, 87, 89, 92, 109, 110] and

Figure 1.4. A typical radiosity scene. This is a replica of the widely used *Cornellbox* which is a box scene with two cubes and a square light source at the top. Radiosity is good at handling diffuse reflection and polygonal surfaces. (See Color Plate II.)

for example, by using bidirectional Monte Carlo ray tracing [57, 56, 108], in which rays are traced simultaneously from the light and the eye. However, these pure unbiased Monte Carlo-based ray-tracing methods are still very time-consuming. An alternative is biased Monte Carlo ray tracing, in which other convergence properties are accepted. Some of the most successful optimizations are in this category. One example is irradiance caching which stores and re-uses indirect illumination on diffuse surfaces via an interpolation scheme [118, 117].

Ray-tracing based techniques are point sampling methods in which geometry is treated like a black box—rays are traced into the model and they return some illumination value. This can be a major advantage in scenes with complex geometry since point-sampling methods only deal with the complexity of the illumination. The independence of geometry can, however, mean that obvious relationships between neighboring objects are not easily recognized, and therefore require many samples to render accurately.

1.2.2   Finite Element Radiosity Techniques

Finite element radiosity techniques are an alternative to ray-tracing methods, in which the equilibrium of the light exchange between surfaces in a model is computed. This is done by subdividing the model into small patches that can form a basis for the final light distribution. The lighting distribution is found by solving a set of linear equations for the light exchange between all the patches.

Radiosity was initially introduced for scenes with only diffuse (Lambertian) patches [29, 16, 71] where it is assumed that the reflected light from each patch can be represented by a constant, independent of directions. Later radiosity was extended to handle more complex reflection models [37, 112, 95, 30, 15, 103], but simple curved specular surfaces are still not handled properly. Basic radiosity algorithms compute a complete view-independent global illumination solution which is useful for walk-throughs but costly in terms of compute time and storage requirements. To improve efficiency the radiosity algorithm has been extended with view-dependent calculations [99], clustering [98], and hierarchical techniques [33]. These techniques reduce the time complexity of the radiosity algorithm by reducing the accuracy in the exchange of light between remote patches, or for patches that are less important for the final rendered image.

The radiosity algorithm is quite efficient at computing the lighting distribution in a simple model with diffuse materials, but it becomes very costly for complex models and models with non-diffuse materials. The high cost for complex models is due to the fact that the radiosity algorithm computes values for every patch in the model. Furthermore, radiosity algorithms represent the solution in a finite mesh, a tessellated representation of the real geometry. The representation can be very inaccurate if the mesh is not carefully constructed, and as a result radiosity algorithms have problems computing sharp features in the illumination—a classic example is sharp shadow boundaries which radiosity algorithms tend to blur. One technique for addressing this problem is discontinuity meshing, where the goal is to precompute the shadow boundaries and construct the tessellated representation accordingly [63]. Unfortunately, discontinuity meshing is very costly to compute, it only solves part of the problem, and it often results in models with a very large number of patches. These properties make the radiosity algorithm impractical for complex models.

1.2.3   Hybrid and Multi-Pass Techniques

Hybrid techniques have been developed that combine radiosity and ray-tracing-based methods with the aim of getting the best of both worlds. Radiosity is good at diffuse reflection whereas ray tracing is good at specular reflection. It seems natural to combine the two. The first hybrid methods used ray tracing to add specular reflections to radiosity [112]—these methods only used ray tracing to include the effect of visible specular surfaces. Later, the ray-tracing methods were extended to compute shadows seen by the eye [88], and light ray tracing using illumination maps [2] was used to render caustics [88]. Visible artifacts in the radiosity algorithm caused several researchers [13, 82, 123] to use path tracing for all types of light scattering seen directly by the eye with the exception of caustics. These algorithms only use radiosity to compute the indirect illumination on the diffuse surfaces. This works quite well since Monte Carlo ray tracing is good at rendering all the details required in the final image but not as good at estimating indirect diffuse illumination in the scene. Indirect illumination on the diffuse surfaces is computed using the radiosity algorithm. The use of radiosity algorithms does unfortunately limit the complexity of the models that can be rendered. This problem has been attacked using geometry simplification [82], in which the radiosity algorithm is used on a simplified version of the rendered model. The simplification is based on the idea that radiosity is used only for computing indirect illumination, which often changes slowly and does not require fine detail in the geometry. This concept is very nice but limited by the fact that simplification of the model often has to be done manually due to the lack of tools or algorithms for simplifying any general class of geometry. A more significant problem is understanding how simplified geometry affects the global illumination in the model, which is necessary to avoid errors in the rendered image.

1.2.4 Photon Mapping

Photon mapping, as described in this book, takes a different approach than the hybrid techniques. The idea is to change the representation of the illumination. Instead of tightly coupling lighting information with the geometry, the information is stored in a separate independent data structure, the *photon map*. The photon map is constructed from photons emitted from the light sources and traced through the model. It contains information about all photon hits, and this information can be used to efficiently render the model in a similar spirit as radiosity is used in hybrid techniques. The decoupling of the photon map from the geometry is a significant advantage that not only simplifies the representation but also makes it possible to use the structure to represent lighting in very complex models. The combination of photon mapping and a Monte Carlo ray-tracing-based rendering algorithm results in an algorithm that is as general as pure Monte Carlo ray tracing but significantly more efficient.

1.3 Overview of This Book

The book can be divided into three main topics.

Chapters 2 and 3 contain background information. Chapter 2 is a review of the physics of light and light scattering as well as the mathematics used to describe light transport. Chapter 3 is a review of the state-of-the-art in

Symbol	Description
x	Position
x'	Position of incoming light
$\vec{n}$	Normal at x (always normalized: $\lvert\vec{n}\rvert = 1$)
$\vec{\omega}$	Direction (away from surface)
$\vec{\omega}'$	Direction of incoming radiance (away from surface)
$d\vec{\omega}$	Differential solid angle ($d\vec{\omega} = \sin\theta\, d\theta\, d\phi$)
(θ, ϕ)	Direction in spherical coordinates
L	Radiance
$L(x, \vec{\omega})$	Radiance at x in direction $\vec{\omega}$
$L(x, \vec{\omega}')$	Incident radiance at x from direction $\vec{\omega}'$
$L(x' \to x)$	Radiance leaving x' in the direction of x
L_e	Emitted radiance
L_r	Reflected radiance
L_i	Incident radiance
Φ	Flux
E	Irradiance
f_r	BRDF
f_d	Diffuse BRDF
f_s	Specular BRDF
ρ	Reflectance
Ω	Hemisphere of directions
$\Omega_{4\pi}$	Sphere of directions
η	Index of refraction
Λ	Albedo
σ_a	Absorption coefficient
σ_s	Scattering coefficient
σ_t	Extinction coefficient
τ	Optical depth
Δx	Small step
ξ	Uniformly distributed random number between 0 and 1
$\xi_1, \ldots, \xi_N$	N uniform random numbers between 0 and 1

Figure 1.5. Frequently used symbols and their meaning.

pure Monte Carlo ray-tracing techniques. This chapter is intended to give an understanding of the algorithms and their specifics, their strengths and their weaknesses.

Chapters 4–9 give a detailed description of the photon mapping algorithm. These chapters describe photon tracing, the photon map data structure, and a number of rendering algorithms including the two-pass algorithm introduced in the original photon mapping paper.

Chapter 10 contains an in-depth description of participating media and subsurface scattering. This chapter contains both a description of the physics of participating media as well as a description of how to use photon mapping to render participating media and subsurface scattering. Chapter 11 contains several tips and tricks as well as ideas for how to further improve and optimize a photon mapping implementation.

The appendices contain information on basic Monte Carlo integration, as well as a full implementation of the photon map.

The most important symbols that we will use are listed in Figure 1.5.

2

Fundamentals of Global Illumination

Understanding the nature of light and how it scatters in the environment is essential to correctly simulate global illumination. After all, global illumination algorithms are trying to mimic the behavior of light in a model. This chapter is divided into three parts: the first part gives an overview of the physical nature of light and the terminology used to describe it. The second part deals with the interaction of light and surfaces and the terminology used. Finally, the third part introduces the rendering equation—the fundamental equation that all global illumination algorithms strive to solve.

2.1   The Nature of Light

The nature of light is complicated and still not completely understood. Many theories have been proposed through the ages to describe the physical properties of light. The Greeks around 350 B.C. believed that light was emanating from the eyes and touching the objects that we see. This theory was not seriously attacked until Alhazen (A.D. 956–1038) described how light traveled in straight lines and was reflected by a mirror. He used a camera obscura (a pinhole camera) as a model for the eye. The next two breakthroughs in the understanding of light were reached by Christiaan Huygens (1629–1695) and Isaac Newton (1642–1727). Huygens described how light can be understood as a wave motion and how this could be used to explain the laws of reflection and refraction. Newton demonstrated how white light is made of colored light that can be separated out (and combined again) using a prism. Newton, however, used the particle model of light and described how light particles are emitted from the light sources and move in straight lines until they hit a surface. Newton published his theory of light in his *Optics* treatise where he argued heavily against Huygens wave model, and since Newton was such an eminent scientist his theory of light dominated for several hundred years. It was not until the early 19th century when Thomas Young (1773–1829) and Augustin Fresnel (1788–1827) began studying effects due to polarization and diffraction that the wave theory gained acceptance [12]. This theory was further established when James Maxwell (1831–1879) introduced four equations describing the properties of electromagnetic waves. Unfortunately, not all was perfect. In the early 20th century Albert Einstein (1879–1955) introduced the use of photons to describe the photo-electric effect, and in 1913 Niels Bohr demonstrated how quantum mechanics could be used to describe the emission and absorption spectra for hydrogen. However, the wave model of light was still necessary to describe phenomena such as interference and diffraction—Niels Bohr called this the *complementary nature* of light.

Currently, the physics of light is often explained using several different models based on the historic developments in the understanding of light. These are [83]:

Ray optics models light as independent rays that travel in different optical media according to a set of geometrical rules. Ray optics can be used to describe most of the effects we see, such as reflection, refraction, and image formation.

Wave optics models light as electromagnetic waves and can be used to model all the phenomena that ray optics can model and, in addition, interference and diffraction.

Electromagnetic optics includes wave optics and, in addition, explains polarization and dispersion.

Photon optics provides the foundation for understanding the interaction of light and matter.

In computer graphics there is an almost exclusive use of ray optics (also known as geometrical optics) and this book is no exception. Despite the name, photon mapping uses ray optics as the fundamental model for light scattering. The interaction of light with matter is based on high-level models that abstract away the actual scattering of photons by molecules and atoms. This means that we ignore effects such as diffraction and interference. We also ignore polarization even though ray optics can be extended to include polarization quite easily [121].

Another assumption is that light has infinite speed. This means that when a light source is turned on, the illumination in the model immediately reaches a steady state.

Despite all these approximations we can simulate almost all of the lighting phenomena that we see around us.

2.2 Lighting Terminology

In this section we will introduce *radiometry*, the basic terminology used to describe light [38]. Radiometry is generally accepted for this purpose, even though *photometry* is also used. The difference between the two is that photometry takes into account the perception of light by a human observer.

2.2.1 Radiometry

The basic quantity in lighting is the photon. The energy, e_λ, of a photon with a wavelength λ is

$$e_\lambda = \frac{h\,c}{\lambda} \; . \tag{2.1}$$

where $h \approx 6.63 \cdot 10^{-34} J \cdot s$ is Planck's constant, and c is the speed of light (in a vacuum $c = c_0 = 299,792,458 \ m/s$).

The *spectral radiant energy*, Q_λ, in n_λ photons with wavelength λ is

$$Q_\lambda = n_\lambda \, e_\lambda = n_\lambda \frac{h\,c}{\lambda} \; . \tag{2.2}$$

Radiant energy, Q, is the energy of a collection of photons and is computed by integrating the spectral energy over all possible wavelengths:

$$Q = \int_0^\infty Q_\lambda \, d\lambda \; . \tag{2.3}$$

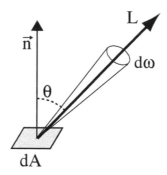

Figure 2.1. Radiance, L, is defined as the radiant flux per unit solid angle, $d\vec{\omega}$, per unit projected area, dA.

Radiant flux, Φ, is the time rate of flow of radiant energy:

$$\Phi = \frac{dQ}{dt} \ . \tag{2.4}$$

Φ is often just called the flux. For wavelength dependence there is the *spectral radiant flux*, Φ_λ, which is the time rate flow of spectral radiant energy.

The *radiant flux area density* is defined as the differential flux per differential area (at a surface), $d\Phi/dA$. Radiant flux area density is often separated into the *radiant exitance*, M, which is the flux leaving a surface (this quantity is also known as the radiosity, B), and the *irradiance*, E, which is the flux arriving at a surface location, x:

$$E(x) = \frac{d\Phi}{dA} \ . \tag{2.5}$$

The *radiant intensity*, I, is the radiant flux per unit solid angle, $d\vec{\omega}$:

$$I(\vec{\omega}) = \frac{d\Phi}{d\vec{\omega}} \ . \tag{2.6}$$

Radiance, L, is the radiant flux per unit solid angle per unit projected area (see Figure 2.1):

$$L(x, \vec{\omega}) = \frac{d^2\Phi}{\cos\theta \, dA \, d\vec{\omega}} = \int_0^\infty \frac{d^4 n_\lambda}{\cos\theta \, d\vec{\omega} \, dA \, dt \, d\lambda} \, \frac{h \, c}{\lambda} \, d\lambda \ , \tag{2.7}$$

where the last term represents radiance expressed as the integral over wavelength of the flow of energy in n_λ photons per differential area per differential solid angle per unit of time. Radiance is a five-dimensional quantity

Symbol	Quantity	Unit
Q_λ	Spectral radiant energy	$J\,nm^{-1}$
Q	Radiant energy	J
Φ	Radiant flux	W
I	Radiant intensity	$W\,sr^{-1}$
E	Irradiance (incident)	$W\,m^{-2}$
M	Radiant exitance (outgoing)	$W\,m^{-2}$
B	Radiosity (outgoing)	$W\,m^{-2}$
L	Radiance	$W\,m^{-2}\,sr^{-1}$
L_λ	Spectral radiance	$W\,m^{-2}\,sr^{-1}\,nm^{-1}$

Table 2.1. Radiometric symbols, names, and units.

(three for position and two for the direction), and is often written as $L(x, \vec{\omega})$ where x is the position and $\vec{\omega}$ is the direction.

Radiance is arguably the most important quantity in global illumination, since it most closely represents the color of an object—this applies to any device that detects light, such as a human observer. Radiance can be thought of as the number of photons arriving per time at a small area from a given direction, and it can be used to describe the intensity of light at a given point in space in a given direction. In a vacuum, radiance is constant along a line of sight. This is a very important property that is used by all ray-tracing algorithms. The exceptions to this rule are the presence of participating media (Chapter 10) and nonlinear media (i.e., where the index of refraction varies continuously [102]).

Equation 2.7 computes radiance from flux. If the radiance field on a surface is available then the flux can be computed by integrating the radiance field over all directions Ω and area A:

$$\Phi = \int_A \int_\Omega L(x, \vec{\omega}')(\vec{\omega}' \cdot \vec{n}) \, d\vec{\omega}' \, dx \qquad (2.8)$$

where $\vec{n}$ is the normal of the surface at x.

The radiometric terms are summarized in Table 2.1.

2.2.2 Photometry

The important difference between radiometry and photometry is that the photometric values include the visual response of a standard observer.

Luminous flux, Φ_v, is the visual response to radiant flux. It is computed as:

$$\Phi_v = \int_\Lambda \Phi_\lambda V(\lambda) \, d\lambda \,, \qquad (2.9)$$

where $V(\lambda)$ is the visual response of a standard observer, and Λ is the wavelengths for the visible spectrum (see, for example, the table from 380 nm–780 nm in [122]).

The *luminous flux area density*, $\frac{d\Phi_v}{dA}$ is called the *illuminance*, E_v, if incident, and *luminous exitance*, M_v, if outgoing.

Luminous intensity, I_v, is the flux per solid angle $\frac{d\Phi_v}{d\vec{\omega}}$, and the *luminance*, L_v is:

$$L_v(x, \vec{\omega}) = \frac{d^2\Phi_v}{\cos\theta \, dA \, d\vec{\omega}} \; . \tag{2.10}$$

Luminance is the photometric equivalent of radiance and often used in global illumination programs.

In this book, we deal only with the physical properties of light and therefore use radiometry exclusively. However, the visual response by an observer can be added as a post-process. This is referred to as tone mapping.

2.2.3   The Solid Angle

The differential solid angle, $d\vec{\omega}$, is used extensively in the description of light. It relates the raw stream of photons (the flux) to the intensity of the light, and it is almost exclusively the integration variable of choice in Monte Carlo ray tracing when the incoming radiance is integrated.

The solid angle represents the angular "size" of a beam as well as the direction. We can think of the solid angle as representing both a direction and an infinitesimal area on the unit sphere. We can express this direction and size in spherical coordinates (θ, ϕ). This requires a base coordinate system (e.g., a surface normal, $\vec{n}$, and two orthogonal vectors, $\vec{b}_x$ and $\vec{b}_y$, in the surface tangent plane). The size of a differential solid angle in spherical coordinates is given by:

$$d\vec{\omega} = \sin\theta \, d\theta \, d\phi \; . \tag{2.11}$$

Here, θ is the angle between the direction and $\vec{n}$, and ϕ is the angle between the direction projected onto the surface tangent plane and $\vec{b}_x$. The right-hand side of the equation expresses the infinitesimal area on the unit sphere as a product of the length of the latitude arc ($d\theta$) and the length of the longitude arc ($\sin\theta \, d\phi$).

Given the spherical coordinates we can compute the direction, $\vec{\omega}$, of the solid angle:

$$\vec{\omega} = \sin\theta \cos\phi \, \vec{b}_x + \sin\theta \sin\phi \, \vec{b}_y + \cos\theta \, \vec{n} \; . \tag{2.12}$$

A frequently encountered expression is the integral over the incoming directions on the hemisphere, Ω. When evaluating this integral it is often convenient to rewrite it as an integral in spherical coordinates:

$$\int_\Omega f(\theta, \phi) \, d\vec{\omega}' = \int_0^{2\pi} \int_0^{\pi/2} f(\theta, \phi) \, \sin\theta \, d\theta \, d\phi \qquad (2.13)$$

2.3 Light Emission

Light in the form of photons is generated at light sources. Sources of light include light bulbs and natural sources such as the sun, fire, and biochemical processes.

The intensity of a given light source is often given as the power or the *wattage* of the source. For a small (point) light source with power Φ_s that emits light uniformly in all directions, we can compute the irradiance, E, at a surface as:

$$E(x) = \frac{\Phi_s \cos\theta}{4\pi r^2} \, , \qquad (2.14)$$

where r is the distance from x to the light source, and θ is the angle between the surface normal and the direction to the light source. This equation is intuitive: imagine a small source sending photons in all directions, where the density of the photons decreases with the distance to the source. The rate at which the photon density decreases is proportional to the surface area of a sphere at the same distance (one can think of each batch of emitted photons as sitting on an expanding sphere). The surface area of the sphere is $4\pi r^2$. The cosine factor in the numerator is due to the surface orientation. A surface facing the source will receive more photons per area than a surface that is oriented differently.

It is common to refer to the color temperature of a light source. This quantity has an exact physical meaning since it is related to the *blackbody radiation*. For a blackbody at a given temperature the spectral radiant flux can be computed using Planck's formula [94]:

$$\Phi_\lambda = \frac{2\pi C_1}{\lambda^5 (e^{C_2/(\lambda T)} - 1)} \, . \qquad (2.15)$$

Here T is the temperature of the object, $C_1 = h \, c_0^2 \approx 3.7418 \cdot 10^{-16}$, and $C_2 = h \, c_0/k \approx 1.4388 \cdot 10^{-2}$, where $k \approx 1.38 \cdot 10^{-23} \, J/K$ is Boltzmann's constant. As an example the color temperature of the sun is approximately 5900K [122].

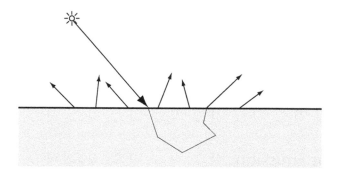

Figure 2.2. When a beam of light hits a material it is often scattered inside the material before being "reflected" at a different location. This general concept can be described using a BSSRDF.

2.4   Light Scattering

When light encounters an obstacle it is either scattered or absorbed. The obstacle can be the surface of a different material or medium. It can also be a very small particle or a molecule, but this case requires special scattering techniques which we will describe in Chapter 10. In this section we will introduce tools for modeling the local light scattering at surfaces: i.e., what happens when a beam of light strikes a given surface. In graphics this is also known as *local illumination*.

First we present the theoretical framework used to describe light scattering, and then we present a few reflection models commonly used in computer graphics. Unless stated we assume that the wavelength of light does not change as a result of scattering (i.e., fluorescence), and we therefore omit the wavelength parameter in our description.

2.4.1   The BSSRDF

When a beam of light is scattered by a material it normally enters the material and then scatters around before leaving the surface at a different location. This is particularly noticeable for translucent materials such as marble and skin, but it happens to some degree for all non-metallic materials. We can describe this scattering using the *Bidirectional Scattering Surface Reflectance Distribution Function* or BSSRDF [69]. The BSSRDF, S, relates the differential reflected radiance, dL_r, at x in direction $\vec{\omega}$, to the

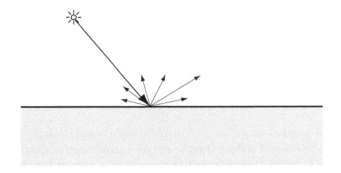

Figure 2.3. The BRDF models the local reflection of light by assuming that all light is reflected at the same location at which it hits the surface. This approximation works well for most materials.

differential incident flux, $d\Phi_i$ at x' from direction $\vec{\omega}'$:[1]

$$S(x,\vec{\omega},x',\vec{\omega}') = \frac{dL_r(x,\vec{\omega})}{d\Phi_i(x',\vec{\omega}')} \; . \tag{2.16}$$

Notice that S is a function of both the incoming position and direction as well as the outgoing position and direction. This is the most general description of light transport. The only assumption is that there is some interaction at some point in space and that some flux incident at some location is scattered to some other location as a result of this interaction. Unfortunately, the BSSRDF is eight-dimensional and costly to evaluate, and it has only been used in few papers in computer graphics [32, 23, 50, 77, 51]. These papers all deal with *subsurface scattering*, where light enters the material and scatters before leaving the material. Even though subsurface scattering is the most common case, the BSSRDF can be used to describe scattering between the elements of a rough metallic surface as well, but this case is typically dealt with in the rendering algorithm.

2.4.2 The BRDF

The *Bidirectional Reflectance Distribution Function*, BRDF, was introduced by Nicodemus et al. [69] as a tool for describing reflection of light at a surface. The BRDF is an approximation of the BSSRDF. For the BRDF it is assumed that light striking a surface location is reflected at that same surface location. This reduces the BRDF to a six-dimensional function.

---

[1]The vectors $\vec{\omega}$ and $\vec{\omega}'$ always point away from the surface. For incident illumination such as $d\Phi_i(x,\vec{\omega}')$ we will assume that $\vec{\omega}'$ is the direction from where the illumination is coming.

This may not seem like a big win, but it enables a series of simplifications that will be described in the following paragraphs.

The BRDF, f_r, defines the relationship between reflected radiance and irradiance:

$$f_r(x, \vec{\omega}', \vec{\omega}) = \frac{dL_r(x, \vec{\omega})}{dE_i(x, \vec{\omega}')} = \frac{dL_r(x, \vec{\omega})}{L_i(x, \vec{\omega}')(\vec{\omega}' \cdot \vec{n}) \, d\vec{\omega}'} \; , \qquad (2.17)$$

where $\vec{n}$ is the normal at x. At first it may seem strange that the BRDF is defined as the ratio of reflected radiance and irradiance instead of as the ratio between incident and reflected radiance. The reason for this is that the change in the reflected radiance is proportional to the solid angle and $\cos\theta'$ for L_i. By including these values in the denominator we avoid having to include this fundamental factor in the BRDF.

The BRDF describes the *local illumination* model. If we know the incident radiance field at a surface location then we can compute the reflected radiance in all directions. This is done by integrating the incident radiance, L_i:

$$L_r(x, \vec{\omega}) = \int_\Omega f_r(x, \vec{\omega}', \vec{\omega}) dE(x, \vec{\omega}') = \int_\Omega f_r(x, \vec{\omega}', \vec{\omega}) L_i(x, \vec{\omega}')(\vec{\omega}' \cdot \vec{n}) \, d\vec{\omega}' \; .$$
$$(2.18)$$

Here $\vec{n}$ is the normal at the surface location, x (note that $(\vec{\omega}' \cdot \vec{n}) = \cos\theta'$), and Ω is the hemisphere of incoming directions at x.

An important property of the BRDF is Helmholtz's law of reciprocity, which states that the BRDF is independent of the direction in which light flows:

$$f_r(x, \vec{\omega}', \vec{\omega}) = f_r(x, \vec{\omega}, \vec{\omega}') \; . \qquad (2.19)$$

This is a fundamental property that is used by most global illumination algorithms, since it makes it possible to trace light paths in *both* directions, as the following chapters will demonstrate. It also provides a simple method for checking if a BRDF is valid by making sure it is reciprocal.

Another important physical property of the BRDF is due to energy conservation. A surface cannot reflect more light than it receives, and the BRDF must satisfy the following equation:

$$\int_\Omega f_r(x, \vec{\omega}', \vec{\omega})(\vec{\omega}' \cdot \vec{n}) \, d\vec{\omega}' \leq 1 \; , \; \forall \vec{\omega} \; . \qquad (2.20)$$

2.4.3   The Reflectance

To quantify the amount of light reflected by a surface we can use the ratio of reflected to incident flux. This quantity is known as the *reflectance*, ρ,

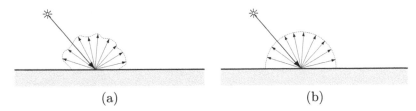

Figure 2.4. A diffuse material reflects light in all directions: (a) shows general diffuse reflection and (b) shows Lambertian (ideal) diffuse reflection.

of the surface, and it is given by [69]:

$$\rho(x) = \frac{d\Phi_r(x)}{d\Phi_i(x)} = \frac{\int_\Omega \int_\Omega f_r(x, \vec{\omega}', \vec{\omega}) L_i(x, \vec{\omega}')(\vec{\omega}' \cdot \vec{n}) \, d\vec{\omega}' \, d\vec{\omega}}{\int_\Omega L_i(x, \vec{\omega}')(\vec{\omega}' \cdot \vec{n}) \, d\vec{\omega}'} . \qquad (2.21)$$

$\rho(x)$ is the fraction of the incident light that is reflected by the surface; the remaining part is either transmitted or absorbed. For physically-based rendering it must be in the range from zero to one.

2.4.4 Diffuse Reflection

A surface with diffuse reflection is characterized by light being reflected in all directions when it strikes the surface. This type of reflection typically occurs at rough surfaces or for materials with subsurface scattering, where light is reflected in some random direction, as shown in Figure 2.4 (a).

A special case of diffuse reflection is Lambertian or ideal diffuse reflection, in which the reflected direction is perfectly random (see Figure 2.4 (b)). As a result the reflected radiance is constant in all directions regardless of the irradiance. This gives a constant BRDF, $f_{r,d}$:

$$L_r(x, \vec{\omega}) = f_{r,d}(x) \int_\Omega dE_i(x, \vec{\omega}') = f_{r,d}(x) E_i(x) . \qquad (2.22)$$

Using this relationship we can find the diffuse reflectance, ρ_d, for a Lambertian surface:

$$\rho_d(x) = \frac{d\Phi_r(x)}{d\Phi_i(x)} = \frac{L_r(x) \, dA \int_\Omega (\vec{n} \cdot \vec{\omega}) \, d\vec{\omega}}{E_i(x) \, dA} = \pi f_{r,d}(x) , \qquad (2.23)$$

since $\int_\Omega (\vec{n} \cdot \vec{\omega}) \, d\vec{\omega} = \pi$.

The reflected direction of the light is, as mentioned, perfectly random for a Lambertian surface. Given two uniformly distributed random numbers

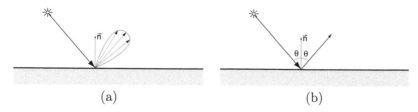

Figure 2.5. A specular surface reflects the incoming light in the mirror direction. (a) shows glossy specular reflection (i.e., a rough mirror surface), and (b) shows perfect specular reflection (a mirror surface).

$\xi_1 \in [0,1]$ and $\xi_2 \in [0,1]$ we can compute the cosine weighted reflected direction, $\vec{w}_d$, for the flus as:

$$\vec{\omega}_d = (\theta, \phi) = (cos^{-1}(\sqrt{\xi_1}), 2\pi\xi_2) , \qquad (2.24)$$

where we have used spherical coordinates (θ, ϕ) for the direction: θ is the angle with the surface normal, and ϕ is the rotation around the normal.

2.4.5   Specular Reflection

Specular reflection happens when light strikes a smooth surface—typically a metallic surface or a smooth dielectric surface (such as glass and water). Most surfaces have some imperfection and as a result light is reflected in a small cone around the mirror direction (Figure 2.5 (a)). The degree of imperfection is often a parameter (such as roughness and gloss) in the reflection models, and these surfaces are called glossy (more detail in the next section). For perfectly smooth surfaces where light is reflected only in the mirror direction we have perfect specular reflection (Figure 2.5 (b)).

The reflected radiance due to specular reflection is

$$L_r(x, \vec{\omega}_s) = \rho_s(x) L_i(x, \vec{\omega}') . \qquad (2.25)$$

For perfect specular reflection the mirror direction, $\vec{\omega}_s$, is:

$$\vec{\omega}_s = 2(\vec{\omega}' \cdot \vec{n})\vec{n} - \vec{\omega}' . \qquad (2.26)$$

Notice that $\vec{\omega}_s$ and $\vec{\omega}'$ both point away from the surface as shown in Figure 2.6.

We can express the perfect mirror reflection as a BRDF by using spherical coordinates for the direction [69]:

$$f_{r,s}(x, \vec{\omega}', \vec{\omega}) = 2\rho_s\delta(\sin^2\theta' - \sin^2\theta)\delta(\phi' - \phi \pm \pi) , \qquad (2.27)$$

where Dirac's delta function, $\delta(x)$, is used to limit the direction in which the BRDF is nonzero (recall that $\delta(x)$ is nonzero only when $x = 0$). Note that $\vec{\omega} = (\theta, \phi)$ and $\vec{\omega}' = (\theta', \phi')$.

The Fresnel Equations

For smooth homogeneous metals and dielectrics the amount of light reflected can be derived from Maxwell's equations, and the result is the *Fresnel equations*. Given a ray of light in a medium with index of refraction η_1 (see Figure 2.6) that strikes a material with index of refraction η_2, we can compute the amount of light reflected as:

$$
\begin{aligned}
\rho_\parallel &= \frac{\eta_2 \cos \theta_1 - \eta_1 \cos \theta_2}{\eta_2 \cos \theta_1 + \eta_1 \cos \theta_2} \\
\rho_\perp &= \frac{\eta_1 \cos \theta_1 - \eta_2 \cos \theta_2}{\eta_1 \cos \theta_1 + \eta_2 \cos \theta_2} \, .
\end{aligned}
\tag{2.28}
$$

These coefficients take into account polarization: $\rho_\parallel$ is the reflection coefficient for light with the electric field being parallel to the plane of incidence, and $\rho_\perp$ is the reflection coefficient for light with the electric field being orthogonal to the plane of incidence. The value of the index of refraction can be found in most textbooks on optics. For commonly used materials: air ($\eta \approx 1.0$), water ($\eta \approx 1.33$), and glass ($\eta \approx 1.5 - 1.7$ depending on the type of glass). Note also that the index of refraction can be complex. This is the case for metals where the imaginary component specifies the absorption of light by the metal (i.e., the fact that metals are not transparent).

For unpolarized light the specular reflectance (also known as the Fresnel reflection coefficient F_r) becomes:

$$
F_r(\theta) = \frac{1}{2} \left(\rho_\parallel^2 + \rho_\perp^2 \right) = \frac{d\Phi_r}{d\Phi_i} \, .
\tag{2.29}
$$

For unpolarized light a good approximation to the Fresnel reflection coefficient was derived by Schlick [85]:

$$
F_r(\theta) \approx F_0 + (1 - F_0)(1 - \cos \theta)^5 \, ,
\tag{2.30}
$$

where F_0 is the value of the real Fresnel reflection coefficient at normal incidence.

Refraction

The Fresnel Equation 2.28 contains the factor $\cos \theta_2$, where θ_2 is the angle of the *refracted ray*. It is computed from *Snell's law*:

$$
\eta_1 \sin \theta_1 = \eta_2 \sin \theta_2 \, .
\tag{2.31}
$$

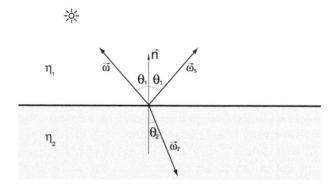

Figure 2.6. The geometry of refraction and reflection.

The geometry for refraction is shown in Figure 2.6. Using Snell's law, the direction, $\vec{\omega}_r$, of the refracted ray (for a perfectly smooth surface with normal $\vec{n}$) is computed as:

$$\vec{\omega}_r = -\frac{\eta_1}{\eta_2}(\vec{\omega} - (\vec{\omega} \cdot \vec{n})\vec{n}) - \left(\sqrt{1 - \left(\frac{\eta_1}{\eta_2}\right)^2 (1 - (\vec{\omega} \cdot \vec{n})^2)}\right) \vec{n} \ . \qquad (2.32)$$

For the refracted ray the amount of transmitted light can be computed as $1 - F_r$.

2.4.6   Reflection Models

Most materials reflect light in a complicated way that cannot be described by the simple Lambertian and perfect specular reflection models. To address this problem several reflection models have been developed for computer graphics.

The early models such as the Phong model [78] were phenomenological models with no physical basis. The Phong model is used to simulate highlights due to either area lights or glossy reflections of a point source. This is done by adding a simple blur to the reflection of the light sources. With the rise of physically-based simulations it was noticed that the Phong model results in a surface that reflects more light than it receives. This problem was addressed by Lewis [62] who derived a normalizing factor for the Phong model.

The first physically-based reflection models were derived outside the field of computer graphics. One of the best known is the Torrance-Sparrow model [106], introduced to the computer graphics field by Blinn [10]. The

Torrance-Sparrow model uses the concept of *microfacets* to explain several observed phenomena of light reflection—in particular the off-specular peaks where light is reflected mostly to a location slightly away from the mirror direction. The microfacet theory assumes that the surface is made of many tiny facets where each facet has perfect specular reflection. The facets are distributed according to some known distribution—for example, one can assume that the average slope angle can be modeled using a Gaussian distribution. This knowledge can be used to compute the local self-shadowing of light by the microfacets, as well as the distribution of the reflected light based on the orientation of the facets.

The Torrance-Sparrow model explains specular-related phenomena (in particular off-specular peaks). It is still necessary to add some diffuse term. For rough diffuse surfaces the model by Oren and Nayar [72] is better. It builds upon a v-groove theory similar to the microfacet theory; however it uses facets with Lambertian diffuse reflection. The Oren-Nayar model can simulate the retroreflection of rough diffuse surfaces such as clay, where local indirect illumination and self-shadowing is important.

Another special class of materials is brushed metals. Brushed metals often exhibit *anisotropic reflection*, where the amount of light reflected depends on the rotation of the surface around the normal. This can be modeled by assigning two roughness parameters that control the slope of the microfacets in different directions. Commonly used is the model by Ward [115] and the model by Poulin and Fournier [79].

There are several other reflection models in graphics. The model by Lafortune et al. [59] supports importance sampling, but the model parameters are not intuitive and are most easily obtained by fitting the model to measured data.

The Schlick Model

A simple, intuitive, and empirical reflection model for physically plausible rendering has been proposed by Schlick [85]. In addition this model is computationally efficient and it supports importance sampling, which is useful for Monte Carlo methods. The model is not derived from a physical theory of surface reflection. Instead it is a mix of approximations to existing theoretical models and some intuition of light reflection behavior.

The model has three parameters:

- F_0, the specular reflection at normal incidence.

- σ, a roughness factor ($\sigma = 0$ is perfectly smooth and specular, $\sigma = 1$ is very rough and Lambertian).

- ψ, an isotropy factor ($\psi = 0$ is perfectly anisotropic and $\psi = 1$ is isotropic)

The σ parameter is particularly useful since it provides a simple way to continuously adjust the surface properties from perfect specular to Lambertian.

Schlick's BRDF is a combination of a specular factor $S(u)$ and a term controlling the amount of diffuse (d), glossy (g), and specular (s) reflection:

$$f_r(x, \vec{\omega}, \vec{\omega}') = S(u) \left\{ \frac{d}{\pi} + gD(t, v, v', w) + sf_{r,s}(x, \vec{\omega}, \vec{\omega}') \right\} , \qquad (2.33)$$

where $f_{r,s}$ is the BRDF for perfect specular reflection as given in Equation 2.27 and $D(t, v, v', w)$ is a directional term controlling the glossy reflection. The parameters u, t, v, v', and w are computed from the surface orientation and the incoming and outgoing directions:

$$\vec{H} = \frac{\vec{\omega} + \vec{\omega}'}{||\vec{\omega} + \vec{\omega}'||}$$

$$u = \vec{\omega} \cdot \vec{H}$$

$$t = \vec{n} \cdot \vec{H}$$

$$v = \vec{\omega} \cdot \vec{n}$$

$$v' = \vec{\omega}' \cdot \vec{n}$$

$$w = \vec{T} \cdot \frac{\vec{H} - (\vec{n} \cdot \vec{H})\vec{n}}{|\vec{H} - (\vec{n} \cdot \vec{H})\vec{n}|} .$$

$\vec{H}$ is the half-vector between the incoming and the outgoing radiance, and $\vec{T}$ is a surface tangent vector in the direction of the scratches on an anisotropic material.

The specular factor $S(u)$ is given by the Fresnel approximation (Equation 2.30):

$$S(u) = F_0 + (1 - F_0)(1 - u)^5 . \qquad (2.34)$$

The directional factor $D(t, v, v', w)$ accounts for the microfacet orientation via two terms $Z(t)$ and $A(w)$, as well as the geometrical constraints of the microfacets via a geometrical term, $G(v)$. These terms are given by:

$$Z(t) = \frac{\sigma}{(1 + \sigma t^2 - t^2)^2} \quad \text{and} \quad A(w) = \sqrt{\frac{\psi}{\psi^2 - \psi^2 w^2 + w^2}} , \qquad (2.35)$$

and

$$G(v) = \frac{v}{\sigma - \sigma v + v} . \qquad (2.36)$$

The directional factor D then becomes:

$$D(t, v, v', w) = \frac{G(v)G(v')Z(t)A(w)}{4\pi vv'} + \frac{1 - G(v)G(v')}{\pi}A(w) . \qquad (2.37)$$

Equation 2.33 contains the three factors d, g, and s controlling the amount of diffuse, glossy, and specular reflection respectively. Schlick suggested automatically setting these factors based on the roughness factor:

$$g = 4\sigma(1 - \sigma) \qquad (2.38)$$

$$d = \begin{cases} 0 & \text{for } \sigma < 0.5 \\ 1 - g & \text{otherwise} \end{cases} \qquad (2.39)$$

$$s = \begin{cases} 1 - g & \text{for } \sigma < 0.5 \\ 0 & \text{otherwise.} \end{cases} \qquad (2.40)$$

To compute a direction for light reflected due to Schlick's BRDF we need to pick one of the modes (Lambertian, glossy, or specular). This can be done randomly based on the importance of each term (techniques for this will be presented in more detail in Chapter 5). We have already described the methods for computing a reflected direction for a Lambertian and a specular BRDF. For the glossy component of Schlick's BRDF it is possible to construct a function based on $Z(t)A(w)$ to compute a glossy reflected direction. The expression for this in spherical coordinates around the half-vector $\vec{H}$ is [85]:

$$t = \sqrt{\frac{\xi_1}{\sigma - \xi_1\sigma + \xi_1}} \quad \text{and} \quad w = \cos\left(\frac{\pi}{2}\sqrt{\frac{\psi^2\xi_2^2}{1 - \xi_2^2 + \xi_2^2\psi^2}}\right) , \qquad (2.41)$$

where ξ_1 and ξ_2 are uniform random numbers between 0 and 1. Note that this expression does not take into account the geometry factor, and the amount of reflected light therefore needs to be scaled by G as in Equation 2.37.

2.5 The Rendering Equation

The rendering equation forms the mathematical basis for all global illumination algorithms. It states the necessary conditions for equilibrium of light transport in models without participating media (participating media is described in Chapter 10). The rendering equation can be used to compute the outgoing radiance at any surface location in a model. The outgoing radiance, L_o, is the sum of the emitted radiance, L_e and the reflected radiance, L_r:

$$L_o(x, \vec{\omega}) = L_e(x, \vec{\omega}) + L_r(x, \vec{\omega}) . \qquad (2.42)$$

By using Equation 2.18 to compute the reflected radiance we find that:

$$L_o(x, \vec{\omega}) = L_e(x, \vec{\omega}) + \int_\Omega f_r(x, \vec{\omega}', \vec{\omega}) L_i(x, \vec{\omega}')(\vec{\omega}' \cdot \vec{n}) \, d\vec{\omega}' \ . \qquad (2.43)$$

This is the rendering equation as it is often used in Monte Carlo ray-tracing algorithms including photon mapping.

For finite element algorithms the rendering equation is normally expressed as an integral over surface locations. This can be done by using the following formula for the differential solid angle:

$$d\vec{\omega}'(x) = \frac{(\vec{\omega}' \cdot \vec{n}') dA'}{||x' - x||^2} \ . \qquad (2.44)$$

Here x' is another surface location, and $\vec{n}'$ is the normal at x'. By introducing a geometry term G where

$$G(x, x') = \frac{(\vec{\omega}' \cdot \vec{n}')(\vec{\omega}' \cdot \vec{n})}{||x' - x||^2} \ , \qquad (2.45)$$

we can rewrite the rendering equation as:

$$L_o(x, \vec{\omega}) = L_e(x, \vec{\omega}) + \int_S f_r(x, x' \to x, \vec{\omega}) L_i(x' \to x) V(x, x') G(x, x') dA' \ . \qquad (2.46)$$

Here we have used the notation $L_i(x' \to x)$ to denote the radiance leaving x' in the direction towards x, S is the set of all surface points, and $V(x, x')$ is a visibility function:

$$V(x, x') = \begin{cases} 1 & x \text{ and } x' \text{ are mutually visible} \\ 0 & \text{otherwise.} \end{cases} \qquad (2.47)$$

We can formulate the rendering equation entirely in terms of surface locations x, x', and x'':

$$L_o(x' \to x) = L_e(x' \to x) + \int_S f_r(x'' \to x' \to x) L_i(x'' \to x') V(x', x'') G(x', x'') dA'' \ . \qquad (2.48)$$

This is very similar to the original rendering equation as presented by Kajiya [52] in his seminal paper, where he showed how both finite element methods (radiosity) and Monte Carlo methods are solving the same equation. Finite element methods use a discretized approximation (of the radiosity equation), and most Monte Carlo ray-tracing methods use a continuous Markov chain random walk, based on the Neumann series expansion or the path integral version of the rendering equation.

2.5.1 The Radiosity Equation

One strategy for solving the rendering equation is to simplify the problem. One simplification is to assume that every surface in the model is Lambertian, so that the reflected radiance is constant in all directions. This means that we can replace the computation of radiance with the simpler radiant exitance term, also known as the radiosity, B. This simplification reduces Equation 2.46 to:

$$
\begin{aligned}
B(x) &= B_e(x) + \int_S f_{r,d}(x)B(x')V(x,x')G(x,x')\,dA' \\
&= B_e(x) + \frac{\rho_d(x)}{\pi} \int_S B(x')V(x,x')G(x,x')\,dA' , \quad (2.49)
\end{aligned}
$$

where B_e is the emitted radiosity.

The finite element radiosity algorithm solves this integral by discretizing it into a system of linear equations [17]. This is done by picking an appropriate basis; a common choice is N elements with constant radiosity which results in:

$$
B_i = B_{e,i} + \rho_i \sum_{j=1}^{N} B_j F_{ij} , \quad (2.50)
$$

where B_i is the radiosity for patch i and ρ_i is the diffuse reflectance for this patch. The *form factor*, F_{ij}, is computed as:

$$
F_{ij} = \frac{1}{A_i} \int_{A_i} \int_{A_j} \frac{V(x,x')G(x,x')}{\pi}\,dA_j\,dA_i . \quad (2.51)
$$

The form factor, F_{ij}, represents the fraction of the power leaving patch i that arrives at patch j.

A significant amount of research has been devoted to solving the radiosity equation efficiently. These techniques have been described in several books (see, for example, [17] for a good overview).

2.5.2 Neumann Series Expansion

The rendering equation cannot be directly evaluated since the radiance value is on both sides of the equation. One way to get around this problem is to recursively replace the radiance on the right side of the equation with the expression for radiance. For this purpose it is more convenient to use integral operator notation in which the rendering equation can be represented using the following compact form:

$$
L = L_e + TL . \quad (2.52)
$$

Here the integral operator T is:

$$< Tg > (x, \vec{\omega}) = \int_{\Omega} f_r(x, \vec{\omega}, \vec{\omega}') g(x, \vec{\omega}') (\vec{\omega}' \cdot \vec{n}) \, d\vec{\omega}' \ . \qquad (2.53)$$

Recursive evaluation of Equation 2.52 gives:

$$L = L_e + T L_e + T^2 L_e + T^3 L_e + T^4 L_e + \ldots = \sum_{m=0}^{\infty} T^m L_e \ . \qquad (2.54)$$

This is the *Neumann series* expansion of the rendering equation, and it forms the basis for several Monte Carlo ray-tracing algorithms (most notably the path-tracing algorithm introduced by Kajiya [52]). An intuitive interpretation of the Neumann series is that it sums terms representing light reflected $0, 1, 2, 3, \ldots$ times. This can be formulated slightly differently using the path integral formulation.

2.5.3   Path Integral Formulation

Using the concept in the Neumann series we can rewrite the rendering equation as a sum over all paths of length k. This gives:

$$L_o(x_0, \vec{\omega}) = \sum_{k=0}^{\infty} \int_S \int_S \cdots \int_S K(x_k, x_{k-1}, x_{k-2}) \cdots K(x_1, x_0, x_{-1}) \times \qquad (2.55)$$
$$L_e(x_k \rightarrow x_{k-1}) \, dA_k dA_{k-1} \ldots dA_0 \ .$$

where $\vec{\omega} = x_{-1} - x_0$ (i.e., x_{-1} is the location of the observer), and K is:

$$K(x'', x', x) = f_r(x'' \rightarrow x' \rightarrow x) V(x'', x') G(x'', x') \ . \qquad (2.56)$$

To evaluate this path integral we need an algorithm that can compute the radiance from any path of length k. This is the topic of the next chapter.

2.6   Light Transport Notation

When describing a light path it is often necessary to distinguish between different types of surface reflections along the path. Heckbert [34] has introduced a compact notation for exactly this purpose. In Heckbert's notation the "vertices" of the light path can be:

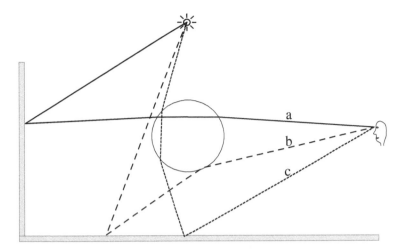

Figure 2.7. The light transport notation makes it easy to classify different paths. In this scene, with a glass ball and two diffuse walls, the paths shown are: (a) **LDSSE**, (b) **LDSE**, and (c) **LSSDE**.

L a light source

E the eye

S a specular reflection

D a diffuse reflection

For example, **LDDSE** means a path starting at the light source, having two diffuse reflections followed by a specular reflection before reaching the eye. Note that we assume that a BRDF can be composed into a specular-like component and a diffuse-like component. For some applications it may be useful to introduce a glossy, **G**, reflection also.

To describe combinations of paths it is common to use regular expressions:

(k)+ one or more of k events

(k)* zero or more of k events

(k)? zero or one k event

(k|k') a k or a k' event

As an example **L(S|D)+DE** means a path starting at the light source having one or more diffuse or specular reflections before being reflected at a diffuse surface towards the eye.

3

Monte Carlo Ray Tracing

Monte Carlo ray-tracing techniques are the most general class of global illumination methods. All of these methods use *point sampling* to estimate the illumination in a model. A point sample consists of tracing a ray through the model and computing the radiance in the direction of this ray. This concept has several advantages over finite element radiosity techniques:

- Geometry can be procedural.

- No tessellation is necessary.

- It is not necessary to precompute a representation for the solution.

- Geometry can be duplicated using instancing.

- Any type of BRDF can be handled.

- Specular reflections (on any shape) are easy.

- Memory consumption is low.

- The accuracy is controlled at the pixel/image level.

33

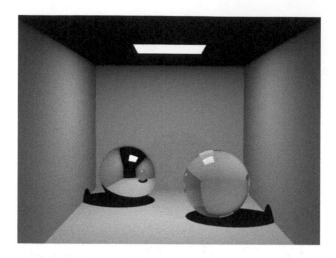

Figure 3.1. A ray-traced image of a simple box scene. The box contains a mirror sphere and a glass sphere illuminated by a square light source just below the ceiling. The ray tracing algorithm can render shadows and specular reflections, but it does not simulate the indirect illumination of diffuse surfaces.

- Complexity has empirically been found to be $O(\log N)$ where N is number of scene elements. Compare this with $O(N \log N)$ for the fastest finite element methods [17].

In addition the Monte Carlo ray-tracing algorithms that we describe here have the property that they are *unbiased*. In practice this means that the only error in the result is seen as variance (noise).

This chapter contains a review of the basic ray-tracing algorithm as well as several extensions for simulating global illumination.

3.1 Classic Ray Tracing

Ray tracing was popularized for computer graphics by Whitted in 1980 [120] with the introduction of the recursive ray-tracing algorithm. Ray tracing is an elegant and simple algorithm that makes it easy to render shadows and specular surfaces. An example of a ray-traced image is shown in Figure 3.1.

The key idea in ray tracing is that light can be traced backwards from the observer to the light sources. In nature the light sources emit photons that scatter through the scene. Only a very tiny fraction of these photons reach the eye, and a naive simulation of this process is not practical. However, we can use the fact that photons move along straight lines

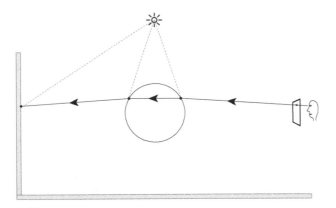

Figure 3.2. The ray-tracing algorithm traces rays (backwards) from the observer to the light. At each intersection point the direct illumination is computed. The visibility of the light source is evaluated using shadow rays (dotted lines). If the surface is specular then a specular ray is traced in the reflected or transmitted direction.

through empty space—that radiance is constant along a line of sight (see Section 2.2.1). In addition we can use the fact that light scattering at surfaces is symmetric (see Section 2.4.2). These two properties enable us to trace light backwards from the observer to the light sources.

The input to a ray tracer is the position of the observer, an image plane (viewing direction and field of view), and a scene description of the geometry and the materials as well as the light sources (as shown in Figure 3.2). The goal is to compute the color (the average radiance) of each pixel in the image plane. This can be done by tracing one or more rays through each pixel in the image and averaging the radiance returned by the rays. The rays from the observer through the pixels are called the *primary rays*. A ray, r, has the form:

$$r(x, \vec{\omega}) = x + d \cdot \vec{\omega} , \tag{3.1}$$

where x is the origin of the ray, $\vec{\omega}$ is the direction of the ray, and d is the distance moved along the ray.

To compute the radiance of a primary ray we must find the nearest (smallest d) object intersected by the ray (this is the object that is seen through the pixel). For the example ray in Figure 3.2, the sphere is the first object intersected.

Given an intersection point, x, we need to find the outgoing radiance in the direction of the ray. For this purpose we need to know the surface normal, $\vec{n}$, at x as well as the BRDF, f_r. With this information we can compute the illumination from each light source by estimating the irradiance at x. As an example the reflected radiance, L_r, due to a point light source with power Φ_l at a position p can be computed as:

$$L_r(x, \vec{\omega}) = f_r(x, \vec{\omega}, \vec{\omega}') \frac{\vec{\omega}' \cdot \vec{n}}{||p - x||^2} V(x, p) \frac{\Phi_l}{4\pi} \, , \qquad (3.2)$$

where $\vec{\omega}' = (p - x)/||p - x||$ is a unit vector in the direction of the light source. The visibility function, V, is evaluated by tracing a *shadow ray* from x to the light. If the shadow ray intersects an object between x and the light then $V = 0$ (x is in shadow); otherwise $V = 1$.

For specular surfaces ray tracing can evaluate the specular reflection by tracing a ray in the mirror direction, $\vec{\omega}_s$ (computed using Equation 2.26). The radiance computation for this reflected/refracted ray proceeds exactly in the same way as for the primary ray. This is the reason why the method is called recursive ray tracing. The recursive nature of the algorithm can be seen in Figure 3.3

Ray tracing is not a full global illumination algorithm. It cannot compute the indirect illumination on diffuse surfaces. Only for perfect specular materials can the incoming light be computed by tracing a ray in the refracted or the mirror direction. In the light transport notation we find that ray tracing can compute light paths of the form:

LD?S*E

In addition the basic ray-tracing algorithm does not compute soft shadows, focusing effects due to camera lens, and motion blur. To simulate these phenomena it is necessary to use Monte Carlo sampling as explained for the path-tracing algorithm.

3.1.1   Algorithm

The ray-tracing algorithm is shown in Figure 3.3. There are two functions found in every recursive ray tracer. The trace function traces rays through the scene, and finds the first intersection point with the scene objects. When an intersection is found, `trace()` calls the `shade()` function which is responsible for computing the reflected radiance (color). This is done by adding the contribution (if any) from each light source, as well as tracing reflected or transmitted rays for specular surfaces.

A practical implementation of ray tracing can be quite complex. For scenes with many objects it is wasteful to check for an intersection with each object for every ray. In this situation it is better to partition the model into smaller regions, and only test the objects in the regions that

```
render image using ray tracing
  for each pixel
    pick a ray from the eye through this pixel
    pixel color = trace(ray)

trace( ray )
  find nearest intersection with scene
  compute intersection point and normal
  color = shade( point, normal )
  return color

shade( point, normal )
  color = 0
  for each light source
    trace shadow ray to light source
      if shadow ray intersects light source
        color = color + direct illumination
  if specular
    color = color + trace( reflected/refracted ray )
  return color
```

Figure 3.3. The ray-tracing algorithm.

a ray passes through. The most common acceleration schemes include grids [100], hierarchical grids [55], octrees [26], bsp-trees [39], and bounding volume hierarchies [53]. An example implementation of a bsp-tree can be found in [104].

In addition it can be costly to trace rays through every pixel of the image. Often an image has regions of slowly changing radiance values (for example, if an object with the same color is seen through several pixels). For these regions it is faster to interpolate the pixel values from neighboring pixels. The decision whether to interpolate the value between two pixels can be decided based on the contrast [67] between the two pixels or the local variance [60, 73].

For a more detailed overview of the ray-tracing algorithm see the books by Glassner [27] and Shirley [91].

3.2 Path Tracing

Path tracing is an extension of the ray-tracing algorithm that makes it possible to compute a complete global illumination solution. Path tracing can simulate all possible light bounces in a model: L(S|D)*E. Figure 3.4 shows an example of a path-tracing rendering of the simple box scene.

Figure 3.4. The box scene rendered using path tracing. Path tracing simulates all light bounces, unlike the ray-tracing algorithm (Figure 3.1). This image was rendered using 1000 paths/pixel. Notice the illumination of the ceiling and the caustic below the glass sphere.

The path-tracing technique was introduced by Kajiya in 1986 [52] as a solution to the rendering equation (introduced in the same paper!). The path-tracing algorithm is based on ideas introduced by Cook et al. in 1984 [21] in the *distribution ray-tracing* algorithm. Distribution ray tracing uses stochastic sampling to compute effects such as soft shadows, motion blur, and depth of field. The path-tracing algorithm extends this idea by stochastically sampling all possible light paths.

Path tracing is a straightforward extension to ray tracing that makes it possible to compute lighting effects that requires evaluating integration problems such as area lights and indirect light reflected by a diffuse surface. These integration problems are handled by tracing a "random" ray within the integration domain to estimate the value of the integral. For example, if a ray intersects a diffuse material then the indirect illumination is computed by tracing a diffusely reflected ray. In the case of a Lambertian surface the direction of the reflected ray is computed using Equation 2.24.

To understand why this strategy works it is necessary to understand the concept of *Monte Carlo integration* (see Appendix A for a brief introduction). In path tracing the unknown function (the lighting distribution) is sampled by tracing rays stochastically along all possible light paths. By averaging a large number of sample rays for a pixel we get an estimate of the integral over all light paths through that pixel.

(a)   (b)

Figure 3.5. The main problem with path tracing is noise. If too few samples are used the rendered image will have noisy pixels. The two images show the same box scene rendered with (a) 10 paths/pixel (see Color Plate I) and (b) 100 paths/pixel. Even 100 paths/pixel is not enough to eliminate the noise for this simple scene.

Mathematically, path tracing is a continuous Markov chain random walk technique for solving the rendering equation [81]. The solution technique can be seen as a Monte Carlo sampling of the Neumann series outlined in Section 2.5.2.

An important aspect of the path-tracing algorithm is that it uses only *one* reflected ray to estimate the indirect illumination (in addition one or more rays may be used to sample the light sources). As an alternative it would have been possible to use several rays per scattering event. However, since path tracing is a recursive algorithm this would result in an exponential growth in the number of rays as the number of reflections increases. For example, if ten rays are used to compute irradiance, and each of these ten rays intersect another diffuse surface, again use ten rays to compute the irradiance then the result is 100 rays used to compute diffuse light reflected twice before being seen by the observer. Kajiya noticed that it is better to focus the computations on events that have undergone few reflections. By tracing only one ray per bounce, the path-tracing algorithm ensures that at least the same effort is invested in surfaces seen directly by the observer. To compute an accurate estimate for the pixel it is necessary to average the result of several primary rays (often thousands of rays).

The only problem with path tracing is variance in the estimates, seen as noise in the final image. The noise is a result of using too few paths per pixel (too few samples to accurately integrate the illumination). Figure 3.5 shows two images of the box scene rendered with 10 and 100 paths/pixel. Such a small number of rays is usually not sufficient to render an image. The rendering of the box scene in Figure 3.4 used 1,000 paths/pixel, and the noise, while still visible, does not distract from the rendering.

Figure 3.6. Path tracing can handle complex geometry, but in a complex lighting situation such as this architectural model it is necessary to use a very high number of samples. This image was rendered with 1,000 paths/pixel and it still contains a significant amount of noise. Even at 10,000 paths/pixel the noise is visible for this model.

1,000–10,000 paths/pixel seems to be typical for most "noise-free" path-tracing images. However, if the complexity of the illumination is high then it may be necessary to use an even higher number of samples. Figure 3.6 shows an architectural model with complex indirect illumination rendered with 1,000 paths/pixel (approximately one billion primary rays for the entire image!). Even with this substantial number of rays and a very long rendering time the image is very noisy.

If the indirect illumination varies slowly, for example, for an outdoor model with a simple constant-colored skylight, then the path-tracing algorithm can be relatively efficient. The Jaguar model rendered in Figure 3.7 is an example of such a scene. The illumination of the car is due to a constant white hemispherical light source covering the model. In this case 100 paths/pixel is enough to get an image with little noise. The reason why path tracing works well in this case is that the function (the light) that we are trying to integrate is slowly varying. Therefore even a few samples can give a good estimate of the integral.

Figure 3.7. Path tracing works well if the indirect illumination varies slowly. This example shows a Jaguar model illuminated by a constant colored hemispherical light source covering the entire model. The rendered image has little noise even though it was rendered with just 100 paths/pixel.

All of the images that we have shown that were rendered with path tracing contain visible noise. Unfortunately it is costly to completely eliminate this noise. As explained in Appendix A this is due to the basic property of Monte Carlo integration that states that the standard error is proportional to $1/\sqrt{N}$, where N is the number of samples. This means that to halve the error (the noise) it is necessary to use four times as many samples! Figure 3.8 illustrates this for the center pixel in the image of the box scene.

The noise and the cost of eliminating it is clearly a problem for path tracing and Monte Carlo ray tracing in general. Fortunately, there are several variance reduction techniques available. If the shape of the function being integrated is known, then it is possible to use importance sampling to concentrate the samples in the important parts of the function. For path tracing this means that if we know where the bright regions are then we can concentrate our samples towards them. This has been done using photon mapping [41] and also by dynamically building a representation of the radiance in the model [58]. Other useful optimizations include stratified sampling in which the samples are placed in cells on a grid. This ensures that the samples are properly spaced, which reduces variance. Properly stratifying the samples is an important optimization since it improves the convergence to $1/N$. For all the optimization techniques the key idea is that all the knowledge about the problem should be included in the sampling strategy. More discussion about this in the context of photon mapping can be found in Chapter 11.

Another very important optimization for path tracing is Russian roulette. Russian roulette makes it possible to trace a ray through a finite number of bounces, and still get the same result as if an infinite number of bounces

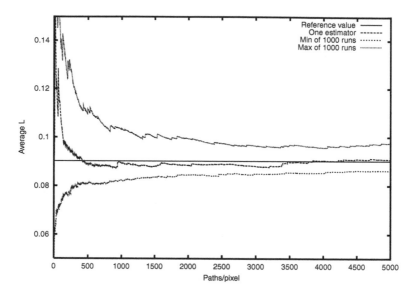

Figure 3.8. Example of the convergence for one pixel (center pixel of the box scene). The estimator curve shows a representive value of one estimator. This estimator is the average of n paths/pixel as indicated on the x-axis. The min and max curves represent the minimum and the maximum average value observed out of 1000 estimators. Note the jaggies on the example estimator curve. This type of appearance is typical; here the jaggies occur when a sample ray hits the light source via one of the specular surfaces in the model. This gives a significant contribution to the estimate and causes a jump in the average value.

had been performed. This is done using a statistical technique described in Section 5.2.4.

For a good general overview of Monte Carlo sampling techniques in computer graphics see [87, 56, 24, 107].

3.2.1   Algorithm

The path-tracing algorithm is illustrated in Figure 3.9. Notice the similarity with the basic ray-tracing algorithm in Figure 3.3. The main difference here is that all rays (not just specular reflections) are traced in the shade() function, and that additional elements for each ray (such as time and pixel position) can be sampled stochastically.

```
render image using path tracing
  for each pixel
    color = 0
    for each sample
      pick ray from observer through random position in pixel
      pick a random time and lens position for the ray
      color = color + trace( ray )
    pixel-color = color/#samples

trace( ray )
  find nearest intersection with scene
  compute intersection point and normal
  color = shade( point, normal )
  return color

shade( point, normal )
  color = 0
  for each light source
    test visibility of random position on light source
    if visible
      color = color + direct illumination
  color = color + trace( a randomly reflected ray )
  return color
```

Figure 3.9. The path-tracing algorithm.

3.3   Bidirectional Path Tracing

Bidirectional path tracing was introduced by Lafortune and Willems [57] in 1993 and independently in 1994 by Veach and Guibas [108] as an extension to the path-tracing algorithm. Bidirectional path tracing traces paths starting from both the eye as well as the light sources.

The idea behind bidirectional path tracing is to exploit the fact that certain paths are most easily sampled from the eye whereas other paths can be sampled better by starting at the light. A particular example is caustics (LS+DE paths). To sample caustics using traditional path tracing, it is necessary to trace a random diffusely reflected ray such that it goes through a series of specular bounces before hitting the light source. This is often an event with a small probability but a significant contribution, and caustics are indeed a major source of noise in path tracing. Starting the path from the light source makes the problem easier, since the light has to reflect off the specular surface, hit the diffuse surface, and then be projected onto the image plane. This concept was first introduced by Arvo [2] when he demonstrated how tracing rays from the light sources could be used to render caustics.

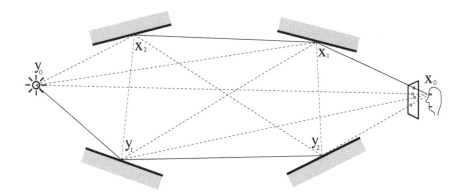

Figure 3.10. Bidirectional path tracing traces paths starting from both the eye and the light sources. The path vertices are connected via shadow rays (dashed lines), and the final estimate is computed as a sum of weighted averages of the different path combinations.

Bidirectional path tracing begins by tracing two paths through the scene: one path, y, starting at a light source, and one path, x, starting at the eye. This is shown in Figure 3.10. The next step is combining the information in the two paths. This is done by connecting all the path vertices, where a path vertex is an intersection point along a path including the endpoints (the light and the eye). The vertices on the eye path are denoted x_i, and the vertices on the light path are y_j. Here i and j are the number of bounces since the eye and the light.

For each vertex-vertex pair, x_i and y_j, the visibility function, $V(x_i, y_j)$, is evaluated with a shadow ray (shown as dashed lines in Figure 3.10). The next step is computing the individual contribution from the light path vertices to the eye path. Here it is important to pay attention to the fact that the light propagates flux, and not radiance. We cannot simply connect the two paths and take the value from the light vertex. Instead the reflected radiance at x_i due to y_j is computed as:

$$L_{i,j}(x_i \rightarrow x_{i-1}) = f_r(y_j \rightarrow x_i \rightarrow x_{i-1}) V(x_i, y_j) \frac{|(y_j \rightarrow x_i) \cdot \vec{n}_{x_i}|}{||x_i - y_j||^2} I(y_j \rightarrow x_i) .$$

$$(3.3)$$

Here we have used the path notation introduced in Section 2.5. x_{i-1} refers to the previous vertex on the eye path, and $\vec{n}_{x_i}$ is the normal at x_i. $I(y_j \rightarrow x_i)$ is the radiant intensity leaving y_j in the direction of x_i. Note that special care needs to be taken when $i = 0$: for $i = j = 0$ the light source is directly visible; $i = 0, j > 0$ is a light ray reaching the eye, and the flux must be accumulated at the appropriate pixel. See [57, 107] for the details on this case.

The radiant intensity, $I(y_j \rightarrow x_i)$, for a vertex on the light path is computed as:

$$I(y_j \rightarrow x_i) = \Phi_i(y_j)|(y_j \rightarrow x_i) \cdot \vec{n}_{y_j}|f_r(y_{j-1} \rightarrow y_j \rightarrow x_i) . \qquad (3.4)$$

Here $\Phi_i(y_j)$ is the flux of the incoming photon at y_j. The origin of this photon is vertex y_{j-1}. $\vec{n}_{y_j}$ is the normal at y_j.

Given Equation 3.3 (and taking into account the special case $i = 0$) we can compute the weighted sum of contributions from all paths:

$$L_p = \sum_{i=0}^{N_i} \sum_{j=0}^{N_j} w_{i,j} L_{i,j} , \qquad (3.5)$$

where L_p is an estimate for the pixel. This equation assumes that we have used perfect importance sampling for all BRDF's (otherwise we would have to scale subpaths on the eye path that do not contain x_0). Note that $i = 0$ will be estimates for other pixels in the image. The weights $w_{i,j}$ must be normalized:

$$\sum_{i=0}^{N} w_{i,N-i} = 1 \quad \text{for} \quad N = 0, 1, 2, 3, \dots . \qquad (3.6)$$

This ensures that the weights for paths of length 0, 1, 2, 3,... each add up to 1.

It is easy to see that:

$$w_{i,j} = \left\{ \begin{array}{ll} 1 & \text{for } j = 0 \\ 0 & \text{otherwise} \end{array} \right. \qquad (3.7)$$

is the standard path-tracing algorithm.

The choice of weights has a substantial influence on the variance of the combined estimate. Veach and Guibas [109] introduced a technique for combining estimators based on different sampling techniques (or different paths). They argued that the power heuristic gives good results for bidirectional path tracing. With the power heuristic the weights are computed as:

$$w_{i,j} = \frac{p_{i,j}^\beta}{\sum_{k=0}^{i+j} p_{k,i+j-k}^\beta} , \qquad (3.8)$$

where the power $\beta = 2$. $p_{i,j}$ is the probability density for generating the path $x_0, \ldots, x_i, y_j, \ldots, y_0$. This path probability can be computed by multiplying the probability of generating each of the vertices in the path:

$$
p(x_i \rightarrow x_{i+1}) = p_{f_r}(x_i \rightarrow x_{i+1}) \frac{|(x_i \rightarrow x_{i+1}) \cdot \vec{n}_{x_i}||(x_i \rightarrow x_{i+1}) \cdot \vec{n}_{x_{i+1}}|}{||x_i - x_{i+1}||^2} .
$$

$$(3.9)$$

Here $p_{f_r}(x_i \rightarrow x_{i+1})$ is the probability density for sampling the direction $x_i \rightarrow x_{i+1}$ with respect to the *projected solid angle*. For a Lambertian surface using Equation 2.24 to generate a sample direction, we find that $p_{f_r} = \rho_d$, where ρ_d is the diffuse reflectance. Note that the probabilities for the path starting points are different; they depend on the sampling technique used for the light source and for the pixel (see [110] for details).

The final image is computed as in path tracing by averaging a large number of estimates per pixel. Bidirectional path tracing uses fewer samples per pixel than path tracing. This is easy to see since a bidirectional path-tracing sample is a superset of a path-tracing sample. However, path tracing may still be faster since the cost of each sample in bidirectional path tracing is higher as it involves the combination of two paths.

The only problem with bidirectional path tracing is noise. Exactly as with path tracing the final image will be noisy unless enough samples are used. For problems with small sources of strong indirect illumination (such as caustics) bidirectional path tracing is much better than path tracing. For outdoor scenes where the observer is seeing only a small part of the model it is often preferable to use path tracing (for example, sending light rays from the sun towards the earth is not very useful). As mentioned caustics are a good case for bidirectional path tracing due to the light path. However, mirror reflections of caustics still represent a problem that is very hard to sample for bidirectional path tracing. In this situation bidirectional path tracing is no better than path tracing. In general path tracing is best when the light sources are "easiest" to reach from the eye—otherwise bidirectional path tracing is preferable.

Another problem with bidirectional path tracing arises when the distance between the eye vertex and the light vertex is very short (such as in corners). The square of this distance is in the denominator of Equation 3.3 and the estimate can become arbitrarily large. This problem can fortunately be eliminated by using the power heuristic (Equation 3.8) since the weights associated with these short paths will be very low.

```
render image using bidirectional path tracing
  for each pixel
    for each sample
      pos = random position in pixel
      trace_paths(pos)

trace_paths( pixel pos )
  trace primary ray from observer through pixel pos
  generate an eye path of scattering events from the primary ray
  emit random photon from the light source
  generate a light path of scattering events from the photon
  combine( eye path, light path )

combine( eye path, light path )
  for each vertex y_j on the light path
    for each vertex x_i on the eye path
      if V(x_i,y_j) == 1            Are the vertices mutually visible?
        compute weight for the x_i - y_j path
        add weighted contribution to the corresponding pixel
```

Figure 3.11. The bidirectional path-tracing algorithm.

3.3.1 Algorithm

The pseudocode for bidirectional path tracing is shown in Figure 3.11. Here the shade() function of the path-tracing algorithm has been replaced with the computation of scattering probabilities for the path vertices. The combine() function resolves the weighting issue and the visibility issue for the path vertex pairs.

3.4 Metropolis Light Transport

The Metropolis Light Transport technique, MLT, was introduced by Veach and Guibas [110] in 1997 as a method for exploiting the knowledge of the path space more efficiently.

The concept in the Metropolis sampling algorithm is quite different from path tracing and bidirectional path tracing. Instead of randomly sampling a function to compute the value of an integral, the Metropolis method generates a distribution of samples proportional to the unknown function. This concept was first introduced by Metropolis et al. in 1953 [64]. For rendering this means that the MLT algorithm samples the image with a ray density proportional to the radiance. This is a useful feature since it automatically concentrates work in the bright regions of the image.

To achieve this sampling distribution the MLT algorithm starts with a random sampling (using bidirectional path tracing) of the space of all light paths in the model. These paths are then randomly cloned and modified (mutated). If the newly mutated path y is invalid (for example, if it goes through a wall) then it is thrown away, and the current path x is used again for an image contribution as well as for a new mutation. If the new path y is valid then it may be accepted as a new candidate path based on an acceptance probability $a(y|x)$:

$$a(y|x) = \min\left\{1, \frac{f(y)T(x|y)}{f(x)T(y|x)}\right\} . \tag{3.10}$$

Here $a(y|x)$ is the acceptance probability of the path y given path x. $f(y)$ is the radiance due to path y, and $T(y|x)$ is the probability of obtaining path y given path x.

By using this acceptance probability the mutated paths will be distributed according to the radiance. This is the basic Metropolis sampling scheme.

The Metropolis light transport algorithm uses several strategies for mutating paths:

Bidirectional mutations: Randomly replace segments of a path with new segments. This mutation strategy ensures that the entire path space will be visited (necessary to ensure convergence).

Pertubations: These include lens pertubations, caustic pertubations, and multi-chain pertubations. Each of these mutation strategies are targeted towards specific important effects such as caustics. If a caustic path (LS+DE) is encountered then the caustic pertubation strategy may be used. This strategy works by making a small change to the ray connecting the specular and the diffuse surface. This makes it possible to sample small localized caustic effects.

These mutation strategies are described in more detail in [110, 107].

For each mutation strategy the acceptance probability must be evaluated. This involves evaluating the radiance returned by the newly mutated path (done using the same techniques as for bidirectional path tracing). In addition the transition probabilities $T(x|y)$ and $T(y|x)$ must be evaluated (i.e., the probability of changing x into y and vice versa)—notice that these probabilities normally are not symmetric.

The MLT algorithm is quite sophisticated and it is particularly good at simulating lighting situations that are normally considered difficult. These are cases where a concentrated region of space is responsible for most of the

illumination in the scene. This can be a small hole in a wall next to a room
with a bright light. Once the MLT algorithm finds a path through the hole
it will mutate and explore this path in order to capture the illumination.
This is much more efficient than path tracing and bidirectional path tracing,
where new random paths are used for each sample.

For scenes with normal illumination such as the box scene that we have
used in this chapter it does not seem likely that MLT will be very helpful.
The specialized mutation strategies will not help much (except for the
caustics) since the entire space is important for the indirect illumination.
Since mutations are cheaper than sampling a complete path it may be that
MLT is faster. For scenes that do not have any coherence—an example
would be the box scene with a grid full of holes in the middle— MLT can
converge more slowly since it will be "caught" in a hole and not properly
investigate the illumination from other holes.

Caustics due to mirror reflections are still difficult with MLT. Even
though the multi-chain pertubation was introduced to handle this case, its
efficiency gets worse as the light source gets smaller, and for point sources
it does not work. Neither MLT or bidirectional path tracing can render

```
render image using MLT
  clear image
  generate N random paths
  for each path x
    MLT( x )

MLT( path x )
  add contributions from x to the image
  if done
    return
  select mutation strategy
  y = mutate path x
  if y is valid
    compute T(x|y) and T(y|x)
    compute L(x) and L(y)
    compute a(y|x)
    if ξ < a(y|x)          ξ ∈ [0, 1] is a random number
      MLT( y )
    else
      MLT( x )
  else
    MLT( x )
```

Figure 3.12. The Metropolis light transport algorithm.

mirror reflections of caustics due to a point source. An example where this type of illumination can occur is the illuminated area of a table as seen through the base of a wine glass.

Another difficulty with MLT is that it has several parameters that significantly influence the variance in the final image. Of particular importance are the probabilities of picking the different mutation strategies. The right choice is highly scene-dependent.

3.4.1   Algorithm

The Metropolis light transport algorithm is outlined in Figure 3.12. The choice of when to stop (`if done`) can be made by comparing the changes to the image as more paths are explored, or by using a fixed number of paths.

4

The Photon-Mapping Concept

The purpose of this chapter is to give an overview of the photon-mapping approach and give some insight into the reasoning that motivated the development of the method. The presentation here is designed to provide an intuitive understanding; the details will be presented in the following chapters.

4.1 Motivation

Our goal is an algorithm that is capable of *efficiently* rendering high-quality images of complex models with global illumination. We want an algorithm capable of handling any type of geometry and any type of BRDF.

Pure finite element radiosity techniques do not satisfy our requirements. Radiosity methods suffer from mesh artifacts, have problems with general BRDF representations (in particular specular materials), and they are too costly for complex geometry.

An alternative to pure finite element radiosity is multi-pass techniques that use finite element techniques to compute an initial coarse solution. The final image is then rendered with a Monte Carlo ray-tracing algorithm such as path tracing (see for example [13]). These two-pass methods are faster than pure Monte Carlo ray tracing and generate images of better quality than pure finite element methods, but they suffer from the limitations of the finite element techniques. In particular they cannot deal with complex geometry since the finite element preprocessing becomes too costly. One paper [82] has addressed this issue using *geometry simplification*, where the finite element algorithm is performed on a coarse representation of the model. This reduces the complexity of the two-pass methods. However, geometry simplification is hard and not an automatic procedure. Furthermore, the errors resulting from using simplified geometry are not understood.

Illumination maps are an alternative to the mesh-based finite element representations, where a texture map with illumination values is used to represent the irradiance in the model. This approach does, however, suffer from the same problems as finite element methods. For illumination maps the problem is computing the resolution of the map. It is also too costly to use illumination maps in complex models, and finally it is difficult to use illumination maps on arbitrary surfaces even if they can be parameterized [19].

The only methods that can simulate global illumination in complex models with arbitrary BRDF's are Monte Carlo ray-tracing-based techniques such as those described in the previous chapter. These techniques have several advantages:

- All global illumination effects can be simulated

- Arbitrary geometry (no meshing)

- Low memory consumption

- Result is correct except for variance (seen as noise).

The main problem with these methods is noise (variance), and, as discussed in the previous chapter, it is very costly to eliminate this noise.

Photon mapping was developed as an efficient alternative to the pure Monte Carlo ray-tracing techniques. The goal was to have the same advantages, but at the same time obtain a more efficient method which does not suffer from the high-frequency noise.

4.2 Developing the Model

To achieve the same general properties as Monte Carlo ray tracing it seems natural to use the same fundamental ray-tracing-based sampling technique. In addition it seems clear that an efficient light transport algorithm must perform a sampling of the scene both from the light sources as well as from the observer. Both the observer and the lights are the important elements in a model: we see the scene from the point of view of the observer, but the lighting comes from the lights. Furthermore, we have already seen how certain effects are most efficient to simulate with sampling from the lights (such as caustics) or the eye (such as mirror reflections).

We want to utilize the Monte Carlo ray-tracing techniques we saw in the previous chapter, but we also want an efficient method. As such we want to exploit the fact that the radiance field in most models is often smooth over large regions. For these regions it makes sense to store and reuse information about the illumination. However, we do not want to tessellate the model or use illumination maps, since this limits the complexity of the types of models that we can handle.

The primary idea for solving this problem is to *decouple the representation of the illumination from the geometry.* This allows us to handle arbitrary geometry as well as complex models.

The second idea is that illumination can be stored as points in a global data structure, *the photon map.* Several alternatives to points were considered, but they all failed to satisfy three conditions: the ability to represent highly varying illumination, being decoupled from geometry, and being compact. In addition points are an extremely flexible representation that makes it possible to handle non-Lambertian surfaces (by including information about the incoming direction of the light) and other information to make the computations more efficient.

The photon map can be seen as a cache of the light paths in bidirectional path tracing, and it would indeed be possible to use it as such. However, it also enables a different method for estimating illumination based on density estimation. Density estimation using the photon map has the advantage that the error is of low frequency rather than the high-frequency noise seen with traditional Monte Carlo ray tracing. This is a desirable property from a perceptual point of view since noise is much more distracting than slowly varying illumination. Finally, the density estimation method is much faster than pure Monte Carlo ray tracing (even if the latter uses the photon map as a cache). The price we pay for using density estimation to compute illumination statistics is that the method is no longer unbiased. This means that the average expected value of the method may not be the correct value. However, the technique is *consistent,* which means that it will converge to the correct result as more points/photons are used.

We use the name *photon mapping* for an algorithm that generates, stores, and uses illumination as points, and the *photon map* is the data structure used to process these points.

Photon tracing is the technique used to generate the points representing the illumination in a model. Since this algorithm is ray-tracing-based and, since the photon map uses points as the fundamental primitive, we get the advantages of the ray-tracing algorithm: complex geometry, no meshing, specular reflections, and more.

4.3   Overview

The photon-mapping method is a two-pass method where the two passes are:

Photon tracing: Building the photon map structure by tracing photons from the lights through the model.

Rendering: Rendering the model using the information in the photon map to make the rendering more efficient.

There are various ways that the two steps can be designed and these are discussed in the following chapters.

5

Photon Tracing

Photon tracing is the process of emitting photons from the light sources and tracing them through a model. It is the technique used to build the photon map (Figure 5.1 illustrates the concept). This chapter contains the details of photon tracing. We describe how photons are generated at light sources and how they are traced efficiently through the model. The techniques in this chapter form a fundamental basis for building a good photon map.

5.1 Photon Emission

Photons are created at the light sources in the model. These lights can be typical computer graphics light sources such as point lights, directional lights, and area light sources, or they can be physically based sources with arbitrary geometry and distributions. Any type of light source can be used.

Just as in nature, a large number of photons is typically emitted from each light source. The power ("wattage") of the light source is divided among all the emitted photons, and each photon therefore transports a fraction of the light source power. It is important to note that the power

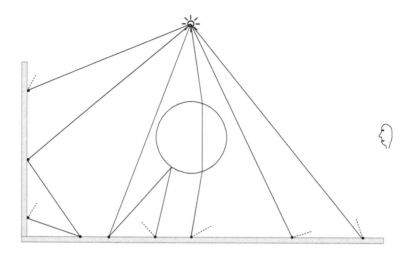

Figure 5.1. The photon map is built using photon tracing in which photons are emitted from the light sources and stored as they interact with the diffuse surfaces in the model.

of the photons is proportional only to the number of emitted photons and not to the number of photons stored in the model (more detail later).

The following sections contain more detail on how to emit photons from different types of light sources. Some examples are shown in Figure 5.2.

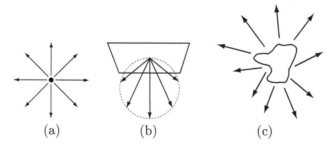

$$(a) \qquad\qquad (b) \qquad\qquad (c)$$

Figure 5.2. Photon emission from different light sources: (a) point light, (b) square light, and (c) complex light.

5.1.1   Diffuse Point Light

The diffuse point light is one of the simplest types of light sources. Photons from a diffuse point light are emitted uniformly in all directions.

```
emit_photons_from_diffuse_point_light() {
    n_e = 0              number of emitted photons
    while (not enough photons) {
        do {             use rejection sampling to find new photon direction
            x = 2ξ_1 - 1          ξ_1 ∈ [0, 1] is a random number
            y = 2ξ_2 - 1          ξ_2 ∈ [0, 1] is a random number
            z = 2ξ_3 - 1          ξ_3 ∈ [0, 1] is a random number
        } while ( x² + y² + z² > 1 )

        d⃗ = < x, y, z >
        p⃗ = light source position
        trace photon from p⃗ in direction d⃗
        n_e = n_e + 1
    }
    scale power of stored photons with 1/n_e
}
```

Figure 5.3. Pseudocode for emission of photons from a diffuse point light using rejection sampling.

To generate photons at a diffuse point light we use Monte Carlo sampling. There are two major techniques for sampling a sphere uniformly: explicit sampling or rejection sampling. Explicit sampling maps the random numbers to the surface of the sphere, typically by randomly sampling the angles of a spherical mapping (see [90] for details). The rejection sampling technique uses repeated evaluation of random numbers until a certain property is present. In the case of the diffuse point light, rejection sampling works by generating random points inside the unit cube. If a point in the unit cube is also inside the unit sphere, then it is accepted as the direction in which to emit the photon. Pseudocode for the rejection sampling technique is shown in Figure 5.3.

5.1.2 Spherical Light

To emit photons from a spherical light source with a given radius we can first pick a random position on the surface (using, for example, a rejection sampling technique similar to the one used for picking directions for the point light), and next a random direction in the hemisphere above this position. For a diffuse spherical light the probability of selecting a given outgoing direction should be proportional to the cosine of the outgoing angle. This is necessary to take into account the fact that the receiver sees the projected area of the light source. See Section 2.4.4 for information on how to generate this direction.

5.1.3   Square Light

Emission of photons from a square light source is similar to the procedure for the spherical light. First a random position on the square is selected, and then a random direction is selected. Similarly for a diffuse square light the probability of selecting a given outgoing direction should be proportional to the cosine of the outgoing angle (Equation 2.24).

5.1.4   Directional Light

A directional light is a non-physical light: no such concept exists in nature. Nonetheless it can be a useful approximation for very distant lights such as the sun. For directional lights we need to know the bounding volume (for example, a sphere) around the entire model. A photon direction is found by selecting a random position within the projected bounding volume. The origin of this photon should be outside the bounding volume. Note that in the case of directional lights, the power of the light source should be given as radiant emittance, so that it is independent of the size of the scene. Each photon still transports flux, but the projected area of the scene also needs to be taken into account.

5.1.5   Complex Light

For a complex light with arbitrary shape and emission profile, the photons should be emitted with a density proportional to the distribution of the light source. Generating photons with a density that matches the emission profile ensures that the power of the emitted photons is the same. This is a good property that gives better photon map statistics (in particular for the radiance estimate discussed in the next chapter).

The simplest way to handle a complex light source is to choose some random position and direction on the light and then simply scale the power of the photon according to the emission profile of the light. This may result in photons that have highly varying power levels, and thus can reduce the quality of the statistics of the photon map.

Another simple technique for handling complex lights is rejection sampling. This works by picking a random photon (position and direction), and computing the probability, p, of generating this photon (the intensity of the light source in that direction divided by the total power of the light source). Another random number, ξ, is then compared with p, and only if $\xi < p$ is the photon emitted; otherwise another random location and direction is selected. This technique may be slow for light sources with varying intensity distributions, but it has the advantage that the emitted photons will have the same power.

5.1.6   Multiple Lights

If the scene contains multiple light sources, photons should be emitted from
each light source. More photons should be emitted from brighter lights than
from dim lights, to make the power of all emitted photons approximately
even. One might worry that scenes with many light sources would require
many more photons to be emitted than scenes with a single light source.
Fortunately, it is not so. In a scene with many light sources, each light
contributes less to the overall illumination, and typically fewer photons
can be emitted from each light. If, however, only a few light sources are
important one might use visual importance [76, 105] to concentrate the
photons in the areas that are of interest to the observer. This is described
in more detail in Chapter 11.

5.1.7   Projection Maps

In scenes with sparse geometry, many emitted photons will not hit any objects. Emitting these photons is a waste of time. To optimize the emission,
projection maps can be used [40, 47]. A projection map is a map of the
geometry as seen from the light source. This map is made of many little
cells. A cell is "on" if there is geometry in that direction, and "off" if not.
For example, a projection map is a spherical projection of the scene for
a point light, and it is a planar projection of the scene for a directional
light. To simplify the projection it is convenient to project the bounding
sphere around each object or around a cluster of objects [47]. This also
significantly speeds up the computation of the projection map since we
do not have to examine every geometric element in the scene. The most
important aspect about the projection map is that it gives a conservative
estimate of the directions in which it is necessary to emit photons from the
light source. A conservative estimate is essential to ensure that we capture
all important effects such as caustics, which can be very localized.

The emission of photons using a projection map is very simple. One
can loop over the cells that contain objects and emit a random photon into
the directions represented by the cell. This method can, however, lead to
a biased result since the photon map can be "full" before all the cells have
been visited. An alternative approach is to generate random directions
and check if the cell corresponding to that direction has any objects (if
not a new random direction should be tried). This approach usually works
well, but it can be costly in sparse scenes. For sparse scenes it is better
to generate photons randomly for the cells which have objects. A simple
approach is to pick a random cell with objects and then pick a random
direction for the emitted photon for that cell [40]. In all circumstances it
is necessary to scale the power of the emitted photons based on the solid
angle of the active cells in the projection map [40].

Another important optimization for the projection map is to identify objects with specular properties (i.e., objects that can generate caustics) [40]. As will be described later, caustics are generated separately, and since specular objects often are distributed sparsely, it is very beneficial to use the projection map for caustics.

5.2   Photon Scattering

When a photon is emitted, it is traced through the scene using photon tracing. Photon tracing works in exactly the same way as ray tracing, except for the fact that photons propagate flux whereas rays gather radiance. This is an important distinction since the interaction of a photon with a material can be different than the interaction of a ray. A notable example is refraction, where radiance is changed based on the relative index of refraction [31]—this does not happen to photons.

When a photon hits an object, it can either be reflected, transmitted, or absorbed. Whether it is reflected, transmitted, or absorbed is decided probabilistically based on the material parameters of the surface. The technique used to decide the type of interaction is known as Russian roulette. In the following we will describe how to reflect a photon off different types of materials and how to utilize the photons more efficiently by using Russian roulette.

5.2.1   Specular Reflection

If a photon hits a mirror surface a new photon is reflected in the mirror direction. Given a normal, $\vec{n}$, and an incoming direction, $\vec{\omega}'$, the reflected direction, $\vec{\omega}$, is found as:

$$\vec{\omega} = 2(\vec{n} \cdot \vec{\omega}')\vec{n} - \vec{\omega}' . \tag{5.1}$$

where the incoming direction is assumed to point away from the intersection point. This equation is the same that is used in ray tracing to trace specularly reflected rays. The power of the reflected photon should be scaled by the reflectivity of the mirror (unless Russian roulette sampling is used).

5.2.2   Diffuse Reflection

When a photon hits a diffuse surface it is stored in the photon map. The direction of the diffusely reflected photon (from a Lambertian surface) is found by picking a random direction in the hemisphere above the intersection point with a probability proportional to the cosine of the angle with the normal. The expression for this is given in Equation 2.24.

The power of the reflected photon is found by scaling the power of the incoming photon with the diffuse reflectance (unless Russian roulette is used).

5.2.3 Arbitrary BRDF Reflection

Given an arbitrary BRDF the new photon direction should be computed by importance sampling the BRDF. For several reflection models the importance-sampling function can be found analytically. Examples include Ward's anisotropic model [115] and Lafortune's reflection model [59].

If the importance-sampling function is not available, then a random direction can be selected. The power of the reflected photon should then be scaled according to the BRDF as well as the reflectivity of the material. Alternatively, it may be better to use rejection sampling similar to the approach described for the complex lights.

Photon Scattering with Schlick's Model

For Schlick's model presented in Chapter 2 we need to pick the type of reflection (Lambertian, glossy, or specular). This can be done using Russian roulette as described in the next section. For the glossy reflection we do not have a perfect importance-sampling function (only for the $Z(t)A(w)$ terms), so this factor has to be scaled with the geometrical factor G as explained in Section 2.4.6.

5.2.4 Russian Roulette

A very important technique in photon tracing is Russian roulette. It is a stochastic technique used to remove unimportant photons so that the effort can be concentrated on the important photons. It is also used to ensure that the stored photons have approximately the same power. This is important for good quality of the radiance estimate that will be presented in Chapter 7.

Russian roulette is a standard Monte Carlo technique introduced to speed up computations in particle physics [101]. Russian roulette was introduced to graphics by Arvo and Kirk [3].

The basic idea in Russian roulette is that we can use probabilistic sampling to eliminate work and still get the correct result. It can be thought of as an importance-sampling technique where the probability distribution function is used to eliminate unimportant parts of the domain. Given a probability, p, that another radiance estimate, L_n, is evaluated we find that:

$$L_n = \begin{cases} \xi < p & \frac{L}{p} \\ \text{otherwise} & 0 \end{cases} .$$ (5.2)

Here L_n is computed typically by tracing another ray. To see why this works we can compute the expected value of the estimator for L_n:

$$E\{L_n\} = (1-p) \cdot 0 + p \cdot \frac{E\{L_n\}}{p} = E\{L_n\} .$$ (5.3)

Here we see that the Russian roulette scheme does give us the right unbiased estimate of L. The fact that we get the correct result even though we do not evaluate all of the problem is important. It means that we can trace a ray through a finite number of bounces and still obtain the correct result as if the ray had been traced through an infinite number of bounces!

In the following we give some examples of the use of Russian roulette. It is often used to decide whether a photon should be reflected, absorbed, or transmitted, and to decide whether a reflected photon should be reflected diffusely or specularly.

Reflection or Absorption?

Given a material with reflectivity d, and an incoming photon with power Φ_p, we can use Russian roulette to decide if the photon should be reflected or absorbed. This is illustrated in the following pseudocode:

```
p = d                      probability of reflection
ξ = random()               ξ ∈ [0, 1] is a uniformly distributed random number
if (ξ < p)
   reflect photon with power Φp
else
   photon is absorbed
```

The intuition behind this algorithm is very simple. Imagine shooting 1000 photons at a surface with reflectivity 0.5. We can either reflect 1000 with half the power, or we can reflect 500 photons with full power. Russian roulette enables us to select those 500 photons. As shown by this example, Russian roulette can be a powerful technique for reducing the computational requirements for photon tracing.

Specular or Diffuse Reflection?

Another simple example is in the case of a surface with both specular and diffuse reflection. The diffuse reflectance is ρ_d and the specular reflectance coefficient is ρ_s (with $\rho_d + \rho_s \leq 1$). Again we use a uniformly distributed random variable $\xi \in [0, 1]$ and make the following decision:

$$\begin{array}{lll}
\xi \in [0, \rho_d] & \longrightarrow & \text{diffuse reflection} \\
\xi \in [\rho_d, \rho_s + \rho_d] & \longrightarrow & \text{specular reflection} \\
\xi \in [\rho_s + \rho_d, 1] & \longrightarrow & \text{absorption}
\end{array}$$

If the photon is reflected, the power should not be modified—correctness is ensured by averaging several photon interactions over time.

Specular or Diffuse Reflection (RGB)?

With more color bands (for example, RGB colors), the decision gets slightly more complicated. Consider again a surface with some diffuse reflection and some specular reflection, but this time with different reflection coefficients in the three color bands. To select the type of reflection we can use the same approach as described in the previous section. For the reflectance we can use the average diffuse reflectance, $\rho_{d,avg}$, and the average specular reflectance, $\rho_{s,avg}$:

$$\rho_{d,avg} = \frac{\rho_{d,r} + \rho_{d,g} + \rho_{d,b}}{3} \tag{5.4}$$

$$\rho_{s,avg} = \frac{\rho_{s,r} + \rho_{s,g} + \rho_{s,b}}{3} . \tag{5.5}$$

Here the subscripts r, g, b denote reflectance in the red, green, and blue band respectively.

Using the average reflectance values we find that:

$$\begin{array}{lll}
\xi \in [0, \rho_{d,avg}] & \longrightarrow & \text{diffuse reflection} \\
\xi \in [\rho_{d,avg}, \rho_{s,avg} + \rho_{d,avg}] & \longrightarrow & \text{specular reflection} \\
\xi \in [\rho_{s,avg} + \rho_{d,avg}, 1] & \longrightarrow & \text{absorption}
\end{array}$$

To account for the fact that the reflection should have used a spectral reflectance value, we need to scale the power of the reflected photon. If specular reflection is chosen we get:

$$\begin{array}{l}
\Phi_{s,r} = \Phi_{i,r}\,\rho_{s,r}/\rho_{s,avg} \\
\Phi_{s,g} = \Phi_{i,g}\,\rho_{s,g}/\rho_{s,avg} \\
\Phi_{s,b} = \Phi_{i,b}\,\rho_{s,b}/\rho_{s,avg} ,
\end{array}$$

where $(\Phi_{i,r}, \Phi_{i,g}, \Phi_{i,b})$ is the spectral power of the incoming photon, and $(\Phi_{s,r}, \Phi_{s,g}, \Phi_{s,b})$ is the spectral power of the reflected photon.

It is simple to extend the selection scheme also to handle transmission, to handle more than three color bands, and to handle combinations of multiple BRDFs.

Why use Russian Roulette?

Why do we go through this effort to decide what to do with a photon? Why not just trace new photons in the diffuse and specular directions and scale the photon energy accordingly? There are two main reasons why the use of Russian roulette is a very good idea. Firstly, we prefer photons with similar power in the photon map. This makes the statistics of the photon map much better. Secondly, if we generate, say, two photons per surface interaction then we will have 2^8 photons after eight interactions. This means 256 photons after eight interactions compared to one photon coming directly from the light source! Clearly this is not good. We want at least as many photons that have only 1–2 bounces as photons that have made 5–8 bounces. The use of Russian roulette is therefore very important in photon tracing.

There is one caveat with Russian roulette: it increases variance on the solution. Instead of using the exact values for reflection and transmission to scale the photon energy we now rely on a sampling of these values that will converge to the correct result as enough photons are used.

More details on photon tracing and Russian roulette can be found in [101, 88, 74, 28].

5.3   Photon Storing

As already mentioned photons are stored only when they hit diffuse surfaces (or, more precisely, non-specular surfaces). The reason is that storing photons on specular surfaces does not give any useful information: the probability of having a matching incoming photon from the specular direction is small (and zero for perfect specular materials); so, if we want to render accurate specular reflections, the best way is to trace a ray in the mirror direction using standard ray tracing. For all other photon-surface interactions, data is stored in a global data structure, the *photon map*. Note that each emitted photon can be stored several times along its path. Also, information about a photon is stored at the surface, where it is absorbed if that surface is diffuse.

It is important to realize that photons represent incoming illumination (flux) at a surface. This is a valuable optimization that enables us to use a photon to approximate the *reflected* illumination at several points on a surface even if the surface is textured (more details in Chapter 7).

Figure 5.4 shows the stored photons (estimated flux density) in the box scene. Notice how the photons estimate the incoming illumination and how the density is higher in regions with strong incoming illumination, such as for the caustic below the glass sphere.

Figure 5.4. The photons stored in the box scene. The top picture shows the box scene, and the lower image shows the photon hits. We used 100,000 photons in this image. The photon hits represent incoming flux in the model. Each photon shows the incoming flux density—the power of the photons multiplied by the local photon density.

6

The Photon Map
Data Structure

The photon map is a representation (a map) of all the stored photons in the model. A fundamental aspect of the photon map is that it is decoupled from the geometry in the model. This means that we do not associate photons with certain geometry, but instead keep them in a separate structure. This chapter describes the actual data structure used and efficient techniques for representing and using it.

6.1   The Data Structure

Photons are only generated during the photon tracing pass. When the image is rendered, the photon map is a static data structure that is used to compute statistics of the illumination in the model. The statistics are based on the nearest photons at any given point, and can be computed at all locations in the model. In order for the photon-mapping algorithm to be practical, the data structure has to be fast when it comes to locating nearest neighbors in a three-dimensional point set. At the same time it should be compact since we intend to use millions of photons.

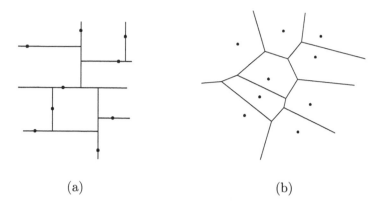

(a)   (b)

Figure 6.1. A two-dimensional point set classified using (a) a kd-tree and (b) a
Voronoi diagram.

We can immediately discard simple structures such as multi-dimensional
arrays and lists, since searching through these for the nearest neighbors is
far too costly.

A simple data structure for maintaining proximity within a set of points
is the three-dimensional grid in which a cube containing the photons is
divided uniformly along x, y, and z into a number of sub-cubes, each
containing a number of photons. A search for the nearest neighbors is
simply a matter of finding the right sub-cube and examining the photons
in the cube and perhaps the neighboring cubes. This strategy is near
optimal if data is uniformly distributed in three-dimensional space. This
is, however, not the case with the photons. Since photons are stored at
surfaces they will be distributed highly non-uniformly for most models.
Furthermore certain important light effects such as caustics can focus light
and thus generate a very high concentration of photons in a small volume.
This non-uniform nature of the photons makes the three-dimensional grid
impractical.

A data structure that is much better at handling the non-uniform distribution of photons is the *kd-tree* [5, 6, 7] (see Figure 6.1 (a)). The kd-tree
is a multi-dimensional binary search tree in which each node is used to
partition one of the dimensions (a one-dimensional kd-tree is simply a binary tree). The photon map is a three-dimensional point set and we need
a three-dimensional tree quite similar to the BSP-tree [104] to store the
photons. Each node in the tree contains one photon and pointers to the
left and right subtrees. All nodes except for the leaf nodes have one axis-
orthogonal plane that contains the photon and cuts one of the dimensions
(x, y, or z) into two pieces. All photons in the left subtree are below this
plane and all photons in the right subtree are above the plane. This struc-

ture makes it possible to locate one photon in the kd-tree with n photons in $O(\log n)$ time on average but $O(n)$ worst time if the tree is very skewed. If the tree is balanced, the worst case time becomes $O(\log n)$. It has been shown that on average the time it takes to locate the k nearest neighbors is on the order of $O(k + \log n)$ [6] which, combined with the fact that kd-trees can be represented very efficiently, makes the kd-tree a good candidate for storing the photon map.

Another efficient structure for solving nearest-neighborhood queries is the *Voronoi diagram* [4, 8] (see Figure 6.1 (b))—the dual of the Delauney triangulation. In the Voronoi diagram each node is linked to its nearest neighbors (the natural neighbors). Locating the nearest points can be done by starting at a random node (point) and then performing a directed walk towards the node (point) of interest by recursively selecting the next node as the one nearest to the point of interest. Having found the node, it is trivial to make a recursive examination of the nearest neighbors. The directed walk can be rather complex in three dimensions and to optimize it one can construct a *natural tree* [119] (which is good for locating a specific node) upon the Voronoi diagram. Voronoi diagrams support queries for k nearest neighbors in $O(k \log n)$ time [4]. Furthermore the Voronoi diagram can provide information on the density of the points—this information is used when radiance is estimated (Chapter 7). Unfortunately the Voronoi diagram requires $O(n^2)$ storage in three dimensions [4] which is too costly for use with the photon map.

Given our requirements for efficiency, the kd-tree seems a natural choice for the photon map. In addition to being a reasonably fast structure for locating nearest neighbors, the kd-tree provides a very compact representation. In the following sections we will give the details of how to manage the kd-tree, including how to balance the kd-tree and how to efficiently locate the nearest photons in this balanced tree.

6.2 Photon Representation

For each photon-surface interaction, the position, incoming photon power, and incident direction are stored.

Expressed in C the following structure is used for each photon [42]:

```
struct photon {
    float x,y,z;       // position ( 3 x 32 bit floats )
    char p[4];         // power packed as 4 chars
    char phi, theta;   // compressed incident direction
    short flag;        // flag used in kdtree
}
```

The power of the photon is represented compactly as four bytes using Ward's shared-exponent RGB-format [114]. If memory is not of concern, one can use three floats to store the power in the red, green, and blue color band (or, in general, one float per color band if a spectral simulation is performed).

The incident direction is a mapping of the spherical coordinates of the photon direction to 65536 possible directions. They are computed as:

```
phi = 256 * atan2(dy,dx) / (2*PI)
theta = 256 * acos(dz) / PI
```

where `atan2` is from the Standard C library. Recall that `atan2(y,x)` returns the absolute angle $(0 - 2\pi)$ of the vector (x, y) with the positive x-axis. The direction is used to compute the contribution for non-Lambertian surfaces [44], and for Lambertian surfaces it is used to check if a photon arrived at the front of the surface. Since the photon direction is used often during rendering, it pays to have a lookup table that maps the theta, phi direction to three floats directly instead of using the formula for spherical coordinates, which involves the use of the costly `cos()` and `sin()` functions.

A minor note is that the flag in the structure is a short. Only two bits of this flag are used (this is for the splitting plane axis in the kd-tree), and it would be possible to use just one byte for the flag. However for alignment reasons it is preferable to have a 20-byte photon rather than a 19-byte photon—on some architectures it is even a necessity, since the float value in subsequent photons must be aligned on a four-byte address.

We might be able to compress the information more by using the fact that we know the cube in which the photon is located. The position is, however, used very often when the photons are processed and, by using standard float, we avoid the overhead involved in extracting the true position from a specialized format.

During the photon-tracing pass, the photon map is arranged as a flat array of photons. For efficiency reasons this array is reorganized into a balanced kd-tree before rendering, as explained in Section 6.3.2.

6.3   The Balanced Kd-Tree

The complexity for locating one photon in a balanced kd-tree is $O(\log N)$, where N is the number of photons in the tree. Since the photon map is created by tracing photons randomly through a model, one might think that a dynamically built kd-tree would be quite well-balanced already. However, the fact that the generation of the photons at the light source is based on the projection map combined with the fact that models often contain highly directional reflectance models easily results in a skewed tree. Since the tree is created only once and used many times during rendering, it is quite natural to consider balancing the tree. Examples of using a balanced versus an unbalanced kd-tree can be found in [44].

6.3.1 Memory Layout

The balanced kd-tree or more precisely left-balanced kd-tree can be represented very compactly by using a heap-like data structure [86]. In this structure it is not necessary to store pointers to the sub-trees explicitly. In the heap structure the array element at index 1 is the root, and element i has element $2i$ as left child and element $2i + 1$ as the right child. Left-balancing the tree ensures that the heap does not contain empty slots. Not storing pointers saves eight bytes (on a 32-bit architecture), which is 40% in the case of the compact 20-byte photon representation. This can lead to substantial savings when a large number of photons is used.

6.3.2 Balancing Algorithm

Balancing a kd-tree is similar to balancing a binary tree. The main difference is the choice at each node of a splitting dimension. When a splitting dimension of a set is selected, the median of the points in that dimension is chosen as the root node of the tree representing the set, and the left and right subtrees are constructed from the two sets separated by the median point. The choice of a splitting dimension is based on the distribution of points within the set. One might use either the variance or the maximum distance between the points as a criterion. We prefer a choice based upon maximum distance since it can be computed very efficiently (even though a choice based upon variance might be slightly better). The splitting dimension is thus chosen as the one which has the largest maximum distance between the points.

Figure 6.2 contains a pseudocode outline for the balancing algorithm [43].

To speed up the balancing process, it is convenient to use an array of pointers to the photons. In this way only pointers need to be shuffled during the median search. An efficient median search algorithm can be found in most textbooks on algorithms—see for example [86] or [22].

The complexity of the balancing algorithm is $O(N \log N)$, where N is the number of photons in the photon map. In practice, this step only takes a few seconds even for several million photons.

```
kdtree *balance( points ) {
  Find the cube surrounding the points
  Select dimension dim in which the cube is largest
  Find median of the points in dim
  s1 = all points below median
  s2 = all points above median
  node = median
  node.left = balance( s1 )
  node.right = balance( s2 )
  return node
}
```

Figure 6.2. Pseudocode for balancing the photon map.

6.4   Locating the Nearest Photons Efficiently

Efficiently locating the nearest photons is critical for good performance of the photon-mapping algorithm. In scenes with caustics, multiple diffuse reflections, and/or participating media, there can be a large number of photon map queries.

6.4.1   Algorithm

Fortunately the simplicity of the kd-tree permits us to implement a simple but quite efficient search algorithm. This search algorithm is a straightforward extension of standard search algorithms for binary trees [22, 86, 36]. It is also related to range searching, where kd-trees are commonly used as they have optimal storage and good performance [80]. The nearest-neighbors query for kd-trees has been described extensively in several publications by Bentley et al., including [5, 6, 7, 8]. More recent publications include [80, 86]. Some of these papers go beyond our description of a nearest-neighbors query by adding modifications and extensions to the kd-tree to further reduce the cost of searching. We do not implement these extensions because we want to maintain the low storage overhead of the kd-tree, as this is an important aspect of the photon map.

Locating the nearest neighbors in a kd-tree is similar to range searching [80] in the sense that we want to locate photons within a given volume. For the photon map it makes sense to restrict the size of the initial search range, since the contribution from a fixed number of photons becomes small for large regions. This simple observation is particularly important for caustics as they often are concentrated in small regions. A search algorithm that does not limit the search range will be slow in such situations, since a large part of the kd-tree will be visited for regions with a sparse number of photons.

Given the photon map, a position x and a max search distance d^2
this recursive function returns a heap h with the nearest photons.
Call with `locate_photons(1)` *to initiate search at the root of the kd-tree.*

```
locate_photons( p ) {
  if ( 2p + 1 < number of photons ) {
    examine child nodes
              Compute distance to plane (just a subtract)
    δ = signed distance to splitting plane of node n
    if ( δ < 0 ) {
              We are left of the plane—search left subtree first
      locate_photons( 2p )
      if ( δ² < d² )
        locate_photons( 2p + 1 )      check right subtree
    } else {
              We are right of the plane—search right subtree first
      locate_photons( 2p + 1 )
      if ( δ² < d² )
        locate_photons( 2p )      check left subtree
    }
  }
              Compute true squared distance to photon
  δ² = squared distance from photon p to x
  if ( δ² < d² ) {                Check if the photon is close enough?
    insert photon into max heap h
              Adjust maximum distance to prune the search
    d² = squared distance to photon in root node of h
  }
}
```

Figure 6.3. Pseudocode for locating the nearest photons in the photon map.

A generic nearest-neighbors search algorithm begins at the root of the kd-tree and adds photons to a list if they are within a certain distance. For the n nearest neighbors, the list is sorted such that the photon that is furthest away can be deleted if the list contains n photons and a new closer photon is found. Instead of naive sorting of the full list it is better to use a max heap [80, 86, 36]. A max heap (also known as a priority queue) is a very efficient way of keeping track of the element that is furthest away from the point of interest. When the max heap is full, we can use the distance d to the root element (i.e., the photon that is furthest away) to adjust the range of the query. Thus we skip parts of the kd-tree that are further away than d.

Another simple observation is that we can use squared distances—we do not need the real distance. This removes the need of a square root calculation per distance check.

The pseudocode for the search algorithm is given in Figure 6.3. Appendix B has the source code of an implementation of this routine.

For this search algorithm it is necessary to provide an initial maximum search radius. A well-chosen radius allows for good pruning of the search, reducing the number of photons tested. A maximum radius that is too low will, on the other hand, introduce noise in the photon map estimates. The radius can be chosen based on an error metric or the size of the scene. The error metric could, for example, take the average power of the stored photons into account and compute a maximum radius from that, assuming some allowed error in the radiance estimate.

A few extra optimizations can be added to the search routine: for example, a delayed construction of the max heap to the time when the number of photons needed has been found. This is particularly useful when the requested number of photons is large.

The Radiance Estimate

Given a photon map we can begin computing various types of statistics of the illumination in the model. We have already seen how the density of the photons indicates how much light a given region receives. In this chapter we demonstrate how the photon map can be used to estimate the reflected radiance at any surface location in the model.

7.1 Density Estimation

The photon map represents incoming flux in the model. Each photon transports a fraction of the light source power, and a photon hit in a region indicates that this region is receiving some illumination from the light source either directly or indirectly. However, based on a single photon we cannot say how much light the region receives. This is given by the *photon density*, $d\Phi/dA$, and to estimate the irradiance for a given region we therefore need to compute the density of the photons.

The first methods using photon tracing [2, 87] used illumination maps (similar to texture maps, but storing illumination instead of color) to bin the photons. Later approaches used a tessellated version of the geometry to store the photons [74]. In all of these approaches the individual photons are not stored explicitly. Instead the power carried by the photons is accumulated for some local region. Knowing the area of this region immediately gives an estimate of the photon density. This approach can be seen as a histogram approach to density estimation.

Density estimation is a research area in statistics, and several books have been written about density estimation problems [96, 97]. It is well known that the histogram-based density estimation approach is inferior to another class of density estimation approaches: the *kernel density estimation* techniques. Kernel density estimation techniques operate directly on the individual elements, in our case the photon hits, and use a local kernel operator to smooth the estimate.

Storing the individual photon hits makes it possible to use kernel density estimation, but it also has several other advantages. The histogram approach is only practical as long as the number of elements is not too large. In addition all histogram approaches so far have been restricted to Lambertian surfaces, where the incoming direction of the photons can be ignored. This reduces the dimensionality of the density estimation problem and makes it possible to use fewer photons. Unfortunately, it limits the simulation to consider only illumination on Lambertian surfaces. We remove the Lambertian surface restriction of previous approaches by storing the incoming direction of the photons in the photon map.

The photon map is decoupled from the geometry. A similar decoupling has not been demonstrated for the histogram approach. Storing illumination in illumination maps or with the geometry represents a tight coupling with the geometry that puts a limitation on the complexity of the models that the histogram methods can handle. In particular the histogram methods rely on a "good" bin size to get good statistics; for complex models the size of the individual geometric elements can vary significantly. For example, in a room the door handle might be modeled very accurately with many tiny polygons. Getting good local statistics for these polygons requires tracing enough photons through the model such that these polygons each receive at least some photons. In most cases a histogram-based approach will risk getting zero photons in small polygons, resulting in no illumination, which can result in black pixels in the rendered image—for high-quality image synthesis this is not acceptable. As a contrast, the use of individual photons makes it possible to get a reasonable estimate of the illumination at any point in the model regardless of the geometry. For the door handle case, this means that we do not need a photon for every polygon, but instead just a few photons to estimate the incoming flux in the region around the door handle. The radiance estimate that is derived in the next section is capable of providing an estimate of the illumination even in situations where there are fewer photons than polygons.

7.2   Derivation

To compute reflected radiance at a surface location we need to evaluate the expression for reflected radiance (from Section 2.5):

$$L_r(x, \vec{\omega}) = \int_{\Omega_x} f_r(x, \vec{\omega}', \vec{\omega}) L_i(x, \vec{\omega}')(\vec{n}_x \cdot \vec{\omega}') \, d\vec{\omega}' \,, \qquad (7.1)$$

where L_r is the reflected radiance at x in direction $\vec{\omega}$. Ω_x is the hemisphere of incoming directions, f_r is the BRDF (see Section 2.4.2) at x, and L_i is the incoming radiance. For this integral we need information about the incoming radiance. Since the photon map provides information about the incoming flux, we have to rewrite this term. This can be done using the relationship between radiance and flux:

$$L_i(x, \vec{\omega}') = \frac{d^2 \Phi_i(x, \vec{\omega}')}{(\vec{n}_x \cdot \vec{\omega}') \, d\vec{\omega}' \, dA_i} \,, \qquad (7.2)$$

and we can rewrite the integral as

$$\begin{aligned} L_r(x, \vec{\omega}) &= \int_{\Omega_x} f_r(x, \vec{\omega}', \vec{\omega}) \frac{d^2 \Phi_i(x, \vec{\omega}')}{(\vec{n}_x \cdot \vec{\omega}') \, d\vec{\omega}' \, dA_i} (\vec{n}_x \cdot \vec{\omega}') \, d\vec{\omega}' \\ &= \int_{\Omega_x} f_r(x, \vec{\omega}', \vec{\omega}) \frac{d^2 \Phi_i(x, \vec{\omega}')}{dA_i} \,. \end{aligned} \qquad (7.3)$$

The incoming flux Φ_i is approximated using the photon map by locating the n photons that have the shortest distance to x. Each photon p has the power $\Delta \Phi_p(\vec{\omega}_p)$ and, by assuming that the photon intersects the surface at x, we obtain

$$L_r(x, \vec{\omega}) \approx \sum_{p=1}^{n} f_r(x, \vec{\omega}_p, \vec{\omega}) \frac{\Delta \Phi_p(x, \vec{\omega}_p)}{\Delta A} \,. \qquad (7.4)$$

The procedure can be imagined as expanding a sphere around x until it contains n photons (see Figure 7.1) and then using these n photons to estimate the radiance.

Equation 7.4 still contains ΔA, which is related to the density of the photons around x. By assuming that the surface is locally flat around x, we can compute this area by projecting the sphere onto the surface and use the area of the resulting circle. This is indicated by the grey area in Figure 7.1 and equals:

$$\Delta A = \pi r^2 \,, \qquad (7.5)$$

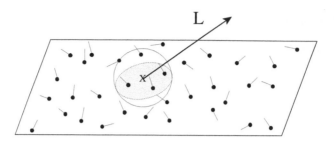

Figure 7.1. Reflected radiance is evaluated by locating the nearest photons in the photon map in order to estimate the local photon density. This approach can be seen as expanding a sphere around the intersection point until it contains enough photons. The photon density is estimated based on the surface area covered by the sphere.

where r is the radius of the sphere—i.e., the largest distance between x and each of the photons. This is equivalent to using a nearest-neighbor density estimation technique [96].

The result is an equation that makes it possible to compute an estimate of the reflected radiance at any surface location using the photon map:

$$L_r(x, \vec{\omega}) \approx \frac{1}{\pi r^2} \sum_{p=1}^{N} f_r(x, \vec{\omega}_p, \vec{\omega}) \Delta \Phi_p(x, \vec{\omega}_p) \,. \tag{7.6}$$

The radiance estimate is based on many assumptions and the accuracy depends on the number of photons used in the photon map and in the formula. Since a sphere is used to locate the photons, one might easily include wrong photons in the estimate, in particular in corners and at sharp edges of objects. Edges and corners also cause the area estimate to be wrong. The size of those regions in which these errors occur depends largely on the number of photons in the photon map and in the estimate. As more photons are used in the estimate and in the photon map, Equation 7.6 becomes more accurate. If we ignore the error due to limited accuracy of the representation of the position, direction, and flux, then we can go to the limit and increase the number of photons to infinity. This gives the following interesting result where N is the number of photons in the photon map:

$$\lim_{N \to \infty} \frac{1}{\pi r^2} \sum_{p=1}^{\lfloor N^\alpha \rfloor} f_r(x, \vec{\omega}_p, \vec{\omega}) \Delta \Phi_p(x, \vec{\omega}_p) = L_r(x, \vec{\omega}) \quad \forall\, \alpha \in]0, 1[\,. \tag{7.7}$$

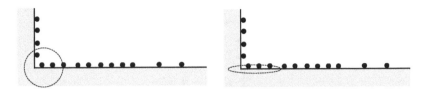

Figure 7.2. In corners the sphere location technique can include photons from the wall that do not belong to the radiance estimate as shown on the left. To avoid this problem the sphere can be compressed into a disc in the direction of the normal.

This formulation applies to all points x located on a locally flat part of a surface for which the BRDF does not contain the Dirac delta function (this excludes perfect specular reflection). The principle in Equation 7.7 is that not only will an infinite number of photons be used to represent the flux within the model, but an infinite number of photons will also be used to estimate radiance, and the photons in the estimate will be located within an infinitesimal sphere. The different degrees of infinity are controlled by the term N^α where $\alpha \in]0,1[$ (the open brackets mean $0 < \alpha < 1$). This ensures that the number of photons in the estimate will be infinitely fewer than the number of photons in the photon map.

Equation 7.7 says that we can obtain arbitrarily good radiance estimates by just using enough photons! In finite element-based approaches, it is more complicated to obtain arbitrary accuracy, since the error depends on the resolution of the mesh, the resolution of the directional representation of radiance, and the accuracy of the light simulation.

Figure 7.1 shows how locating the nearest photons is equivalent to expanding a sphere around x and using the photons within this sphere. It is possible to use other volumes than the sphere in this process. One might use a cube instead, a cylinder, or perhaps a disc. This could be useful to obtain an algorithm that is either faster at locating the nearest photons or perhaps more accurate in the selection of photons. If a different volume is used, then ΔA in Equation 7.4 should be replaced by the area of the intersection between the volume and the tangent plane touching the surface at x. The sphere has the obvious advantage that the projected area and the distance computations are very simple and thus efficiently computed. A more accurate volume can be obtained by modifying the sphere into a disc (ellipsoid) by compressing the sphere in the direction of the surface normal at x (shown in Figure 7.2) [43]. The advantage of using a disc would be that fewer "false photons" are used in the estimate at edges and in corners. This modification works pretty well at the edges in a room, for instance, since it prevents photons on the walls from leaking down to the floor. One

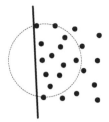

Figure 7.3. If the radiance estimate is computed close to a wall, then the projected area of the disc may not correctly represent the true area covered by the photons. This problem can be eliminated by computing the convex hull of the photons or, alternatively, it can be reduced via filtering.

issue that still occurs, however, is that the area estimate might be wrong or photons may leak into areas where they do not belong. As illustrated in Figure 7.3, this is the case at edges where a large part of the disc is inside the wall. The projected area does not truly reflect the photon density in this case. One way to eliminate this problem is to compute the convex hull of the photons (there are several standard algorithms for this purpose [86]). A simpler strategy is the use of filtering, which will be described later in this chapter.

7.3 Algorithm

The pseudocode for computing the radiance estimate is shown in Figure 7.4. It is a straightforward implementation of Equation 7.6. For Lambertian surfaces the code can be simplified further. The BRDF evaluation $f_r(x, \vec{\omega}', \vec{p_d})$ can then be replaced with a simple dot product comparison to exclude photons hitting the backside of the surface.

7.4 Filtering

If the number of photons in the photon map is too low, the radiance estimates become blurry at the edges of sharp features in the illumination. This artifact can be pleasing when the photon map is used to estimate indirect illumination for a distribution ray tracer (see Chapter 9 and Figure 9.7), but it is unwanted in situations where the radiance estimate represents caustics. Caustics often have sharp edges, and it would be nice to preserve these edges without requiring too many photons.

```
radiance_estimate( x, ω⃗', n⃗ ) {
    locate n nearest photons
    r = distance to the nth nearest photon
    Σflux = 0
    for each photon p do {
        p⃗d = photon direction
        Φp = photon power
        Σflux += fr(x,ω⃗',p⃗d) * Φp
    }
    Lr = Σflux/(πr²)
    return Lr
}
```

Figure 7.4. Pseudocode for computing a radiance estimate for an incoming ray with direction $\vec{\omega}'$ hitting a surface location x with normal $\vec{n}$. The n nearest photons are located and evaluated using Equation 7.6.

To reduce the amount of blur at edges, the radiance estimate can be filtered. The idea behind filtering is to increase the weight of photons that are close to the point of interest, x. Since we use a sphere to locate the photons, it would be natural to assume that the filters should be three-dimensional. However, photons are stored at surfaces, which are two-dimensional. The area estimate is also based on the assumption that photons are located on a surface. We therefore need a two-dimensional filter (similar to image filters) which is normalized over the region defined by the photons.

The idea of filtering caustics is not new. Collins [18] has examined several filters in combination with illumination maps. The filters described in the following are two radially symmetric filters: the cone filter and the Gaussian filter [43], and the specialized differential filter introduced in [47]. For examples of more advanced filters see [68].

7.4.1 The Cone Filter

The cone filter [43] assigns a weight, w_{pc}, to each photon based on the distance, d_p, between x and the photon p. This weight is:

$$w_{pc} = 1 - \frac{d_p}{k\,r}, \tag{7.8}$$

where $k \geq 1$ is a filter constant characterizing the filter and r is the maximum distance. The normalization of the filter based on a two-dimensional

Figure 7.5. The caustic from a lens on a cube using 10,000 photons. The left image is the unfiltered radiance estimate and has some blur at the edges. The right image shows the result of using the cone filter with $k = 1.1$—note how the edges are much sharper and more well-defined.

distribution of the photons is $1 - \frac{2}{3k}$ and the filtered radiance estimate becomes:

$$L_r(x, \vec{\omega}) \approx \frac{\sum_{p=1}^{N} f_r(x, \vec{\omega}_p, \vec{\omega}) \Delta \Phi_p(x, \vec{\omega}_p) w_{pc}}{(1 - \frac{2}{3k}) \pi r^2}. \tag{7.9}$$

The effect of the cone filter is illustrated in Figure 7.5.

7.4.2 The Gaussian Filter

The Gaussian filter [43] has previously been reported to give good results when filtering caustics in illumination maps [18]. It is easy to use the Gaussian filter with the photon map since we do not need to warp the filter to some surface function. Instead we use the assumption about the locally flat surfaces, and we can use a simple Gaussian filter [75]; the weight w_{pg} of each photon becomes

$$w_{pg} = \alpha \left[1 - \frac{1 - e^{-\beta \frac{d_p^2}{2r^2}}}{1 - e^{-\beta}} \right], \tag{7.10}$$

where d_p is the distance between the photon p and x and $\alpha = 1.818$ and $\beta = 1.953$ (see [75] for details). This filter is normalized, and the only change to Equation 7.6 is that each photon contribution is multiplied by w_{pg}:

$$L_r(x, \vec{\omega}) \approx \sum_{p=1}^{N} \frac{1}{\pi r^2} f_r(x, \vec{\omega}_p, \vec{\omega}) \Delta \Phi_p(x, \vec{\omega}_p) w_{pg}. \tag{7.11}$$

7.4.3   Differential Checking

The differential checking approach is a technique for deciding how many photons to include in the radiance estimate [47]. The idea is to detect regions near edges in the estimation process and use fewer photons in these regions. This may result in noise near the edges, but that is often preferable to blurry edges.

The radiance estimate is modified based on the following observation: when adding photons to the estimate, near an edge the changes of the estimate will be monotonic. For example, if we are just outside a caustic and we begin to add photons to the estimate (by increasing the size of the sphere centered at x that contains the photons), then it can be observed that the value of the estimate is increasing as we add more photons—and vice versa when we are inside the caustic. Based on this observation, differential checking can be added to the estimate—we stop adding photons and use the estimate available if we observe that the estimate is either constantly increasing or decreasing as more photons are added. In practice this can be a bit tricky to control, and in general the cone filter or the Gaussian filter are better to use.

7.5   Photon Gathering

The radiance estimate derived in this chapter uses density estimation to compute reflected radiance from the photon map. This is not the only method by which radiance can be estimated from the photon map.

Another approach which does not use density estimation is to consider each photon as a light source (it is necessary to include the BRDF at the position where the photon is stored). Photons that have been reflected n times before being stored represent $n + 1$ bounces of indirect illumination.

To compute reflected radiance at a given point the photon map is simply used as a collection of lights in addition to the real light sources in the model. Each light source and photon is sampled to compute the contribution to the reflected radiance. Since the photon map typically stores more than 100,000 photons, this approach is very costly. It can be optimized by randomly selecting photons instead of sampling all of them. This could also be done using importance sampling by finding the most important photons.

This photon gathering approach can be seen as a special case of bidirectional path tracing where light rays are traced through multiple bounces. The intersection locations of these light rays are cached and re-used multiple times.

8

Visualizing the Photon Map

The radiance estimate derived in the previous chapter allows us to begin rendering images. The first step is building a photon map using photon tracing as described in Chapter 5. This photon map can then be visualized directly (via the radiance estimate) by using a simplified ray tracer. This ray tracer uses the radiance estimate to compute the reflected radiance from all diffuse materials and standard recursive ray tracing for specular materials. This is illustrated in Figure 8.1.

Is this simple visualization a full solution to the rendering equation? To answer this question we can look at the paths traced by the photons and the rays and see if they cover the space of all paths.

L(S|D)*D are all the paths represented by the photon map.

(LS*E)|(DS*E) are all the paths traced by the ray tracer.

The combination of these paths shows that the method does indeed trace all paths between the eye and the light source. Pure ray tracing handles the case where the light is directly visible or seen through one or more specular

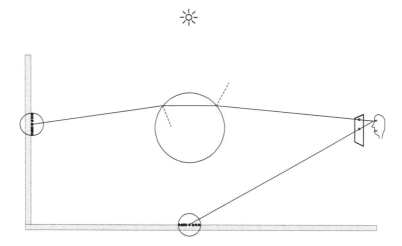

Figure 8.1. The photon map can be visualized directly using a simple ray tracer. For all diffuse surfaces the ray tracer uses the radiance estimate from the photon map, whereas standard recursive ray tracing is used for specular surfaces.

reflections. The photon map combined with the ray tracer handles all the cases where there is at least one diffuse reflection between the eye and the light source. In particular, this approach can be used to render caustics efficiently.

8.1   Rendering Caustics

Caustics are formed when light reflected from or transmitted through one or more specular surfaces strikes a diffuse surface. As discussed in Chapter 3, caustics and reflections of caustics are particularly difficult to handle with standard Monte Carlo ray-tracing techniques. In contrast caustics are very easy to compute using photon mapping.

In Figure 8.2 we see a simple example of a caustic. It is a glass ball on a wood table. When light illuminates the glass ball, it is focused through the ball and it forms a concentrated spot of light, a caustic, on the table.

We can simulate just the caustics by storing only the photons that have been reflected or transmitted by the glass ball. The result of this caustics simulation is shown in Figure 8.2 (a). This example uses just 10,000 photons in the photon map. Note that even this relatively small number of photons results in a nice focused caustic, and it is very fast to render.

(a)   (b)

Figure 8.2. A caustic is formed as light is focused through a glass ball onto a wood table. Image (a) was rendered using photon mapping, and (b) was rendered using path tracing.

In comparison Figure 8.2 (b) shows the same glass ball scene rendered using path tracing with 1000 paths/pixel. Even with this large number of rays and a rendering time that is several hundred times longer than for the photon mapping example, we still get a very noisy caustic. This illustrates the observation in Chapter 3 that Monte Carlo ray-tracing techniques have problems simulating caustics and their mirror reflections (as seen in the glass ball).

8.2   Rendering Color Bleeding

Having seen the success by which we could render caustics it seems natural to try using the same approach to render other types of illumination, such as color bleeding. Color bleeding is a result of light exchange between diffuse surfaces—an example is the red glow on a white wall due to light reflected off an adjacent red carpet. This type of illumination has typically been simulated with finite element algorithms.

With photon mapping we can use the exact same approach as for caustics. The result of such a simulation on the simple box scene is shown in Figure 8.3.

Figure 8.3 (a) shows a simulation using just 10,000 photons in the photon map and 100 photons in the radiance estimate. Even this small number of photons gives a reasonable estimate of the overall illumination in the box (compared with the reference image in Figure 9.9). However, using only 10,000 photons does give a number of unwanted artifacts, such as the lack of detail as well as a bumpy appearance due to variance in the radiance estimate. Compared to the 1,000,000 pixels in the rendered image,

(a)   (b)

Figure 8.3. The box scene simulated using a direct visualization of the photon map. Image (a) uses 10,000 photons in the photon map and 100 in the radiance estimate, and image (b) uses 500,000 in the photon map and 500 in the radiance estimate.

10,000 photons is a low number, and it is sufficiently low that the assumption about the surface being locally flat is no longer valid. A workaround could be to remove this assumption and try estimating the photon density using more accurate techniques. Another approach could be simply using more photons.

A simulation with 500,000 photons in the photon map and 500 in the radiance estimate is shown in Figure 8.3 (b). This image is clearly better than the previous image with 10,000 photons. There is better detail, and the artifacts along the edges have been reduced significantly.

To improve the results further one can use more photons. This strategy has been advocated in a number of papers [93, 113] under the name *density estimation*. To obtain good quality these techniques often use more than 100 million photons and more than 10,000 photons in the density estimate. Due to this extreme number of photons, the underlying structures are different from those used in the photon map. Density estimation uses a large file on a local hard disk to store all the photons. Each photon is stored with just a hit position within a given triangle. This data can be represented using just six bytes, and this makes it possible to store more than 100 million photons. The photons are later processed per triangle in order to estimate irradiance (only for Lambertian surfaces since the incoming direction of the photon is not stored). The density estimation algorithm can be used to capture fine detail in caustics and indirect illumination, but the processing time is very high. Tracing and processing several hundred million photons takes several hours or even days for complex scenes. Furthermore, it would be even more costly to include non-diffuse surfaces in the algorithm. But

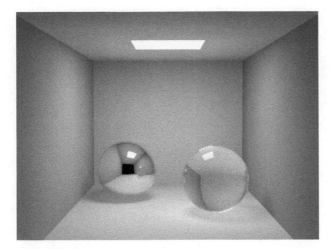

Figure 8.4. A simulation of global illumination in the box using 10,000 photons in the photon map and 500 photons in the radiance estimate. For this image we used only the photon map to compute the indirect illumination. The direct lighting is computed using standard ray-tracing techniques. Even though the indirect lighting is blurry (in particular the caustic below the glass sphere) the overall quality of the illumination is reasonable.

for complex scenes with diffuse surfaces, density estimation can be used to compute accurate walkthrough solutions [113], and for this purpose it is probably more practical than finite element methods.

8.2.1   Excluding Direct Illumination

Another technique for improving the accuracy of the rendered image is to use the photon map only for indirect illumination, and then use ray tracing to compute the direct illumination. This is similar to strategies used for radiosity [87] to improve the accuracy of shadow boundaries. For scenes that are dominated by indirect illumination this approach is less useful, and a large number of photons may still be necessary for accurate simulations. But for simple scenes it does give a relatively practical approach that is fairly robust. See Figure 8.4 for an example of this approach.

8.3   Fast Approximations

In the previous section it was shown how increasing the number of photons in the photon map can be used to simulate color bleeding accurately.

Figure 8.5. A fast simulation of the box scene. This example was rendered faster than just using ray tracing. The trick is to use only 200 photons in the photon map and 50 in the radiance estimate. A consequence of this simple approximation is that the illumination is very blurry (even the shadows are missing).

Increasing the number of photons does, however, increase both the time it takes to build the photon map and the time it takes to render the image. What if we are just interested in an approximate representation of the indirect illumination? Can we go in the other direction using fewer photons and get fast results? One technique for obtaining a fast approximation is to use very few photons. This results in a blurry estimate, which for some applications may be acceptable.

Figure 8.5 shows a simulation of the box scene using just 200 photons in the photon map and 50 photons in the radiance estimate. The illumination is very blurry and as a consequence the shadows and the caustics are missing, but the overall illumination is approximately correct, and this visualization is representative of the final rendering shown in Figure 9.9. This image was rendered faster than the ray-tracing image, and the main reason is that we are using ray tracing only to compute the first intersection and the mirror reflections and transmissions. The cost of using the photon map is almost negligible in this example.

Another fast visualization technique [68, 111] for walkthroughs computes irradiance from the photons only at the vertices of a mesh. The photons can also be used to refine the mesh where necessary.

Figure 8.6. Cardioid-shaped caustic due to reflection inside a metal ring.

8.4 Caustics Examples

As shown in this chapter, directly visualizing the photon map works best for caustics, and the examples for this chapter are all related to caustics.

8.4.1 Reflection Inside a Ring

Figure 8.6 shows a caustic formed on a table due to light reflected inside a metal ring. This cardioid-shaped caustic can be observed very often among real objects—for example, on the bottom of a coffee cup or by placing a metal ring on a table. The caustic was simulated using 50,000 photons. The reason why we can use this relatively small number of photons is that they are stored where the caustic is most intense.

8.4.2 Prism with Dispersion

The classic example of dispersion with a glass prism is shown in Figure 8.7. Here dispersion is simulated by using a different index of refraction for each of the three "wavelengths" corresponding to red, green, and blue. Even though only three separate wavelengths have been sampled, the color variations in the caustics are smooth. An accurate color representation would require more wavelength samples; such an extension to the photon map is easy to implement. 500,000 photons were used in the caustics and 80 photons were used in the radiance estimate.

Figure 8.7. Caustics through a prism with dispersion.

8.4.3   Caustics on a Non-Lambertian Surface

Figure 8.8 shows one of the standard models used to illustrate caustics. The cardioid caustic is formed by placing a light source on the edge of a cylinder which has a reflective inner side. The incoming direction of the light at the edge of the cardioid equals the tangent to the cardioid. This information is useful for analyzing the changes as we change the reflective properties of the receiving surface. It allows us to predict how the caustic should look as the surface becomes more glossy. The figure contains four rendered images showing how the caustic looks as we change the roughness (using Schlick's reflection model) of the surface from 1 to 0.01. As expected the intensity of the caustic is reduced most greatly in those parts where the incoming direction of the light differs most from the incoming direction of the viewing ray. We used approximately 340,000 photons in all four images corresponding to 7 MB of memory.

8.4.4   A Glass of Cognac on a Rough Surface

Figure 8.9 demonstrates the caustic from a glass of cognac onto a sand surface. The sand is a procedural surface (with 2^{21} triangles) with a synthetic sand texture. We used Schlick's reflection model with $\sigma = 0.6$ for the sand—using a Lambertian approximation makes the sand look more unnatural and flat.

Figure 8.8. Four images demonstrating the looks of the cardioid caustic created as light is reflected inside a cylinder ring. The receiving surface is changed from Lambertian (top left) to glossy specular (lower right). For this purpose we used Schlick's reflection model with $\sigma = 1.0$, 0.5, 0.1, and 0.01 (from top left to lower right).

Figure 8.9. A glass of cognac on a sand surface. The sand is a fractal surface with a synthetic sand texture. Schlick's reflection model with a roughness $\sigma = 0.6$ was used for the sand. (See Color Plate IV.)

Figure 8.10. Close-up of the caustic in Figure 8.9. Notice that all of the illuminated area below the glass is part of the caustic. The shadow boundary below the cognac glass is simulated with the photon map whereas the shadow outside the glass is computed using standard ray-tracing techniques. (See Color Plate V.)

The caustic in this image was rendered using approximately 350,000 photons. Notice how the red-looking caustic is formed as light is transmitted through several layers of glass and cognac. The intensity of each photon is modified based on the distance it moves through the glass and cognac media (using Beer's law). Figure 8.10 is a close-up of the caustic in Figure 8.9.

9

A Practical
Two-Pass Algorithm

In the previous chapters a number of tools and techniques were developed for building and using a photon map. In this chapter we show how to combine these techniques into an efficient and practical two-pass algorithm [42]. In this chapter we will ignore the presence of participating media (techniques for handling participating media are presented in Chapter 10).

9.1 Overview

The two steps in the algorithm are:

Pass 1 : Building the photon maps using photon tracing.

Pass 2 : Rendering using these photon maps.

Unlike the previous chapter, the rendering method here is a distribution ray tracer that computes both the direct and the indirect illumination (except for caustics). This makes it possible to render accurate images using a small number of photons.

We first show mathematically how to split the rendering equation into several components that can be computed separately. In the following sections, we describe how each of these components can be evaluated efficiently.

9.2   Solving the Rendering Equation

As shown in Section 2.5 the outgoing radiance, L_o, at a given surface location, x, can be computed as:

$$L_o(x, \vec{\omega}) = L_e(x, \vec{\omega}) + L_r(x, \vec{\omega}) \,, \tag{9.1}$$

where the reflected radiance, L_r, is computed by the following integral:

$$L_r(x, \vec{\omega}) = \int_{\Omega} f_r(x, \vec{\omega}', \vec{\omega}) L_i(x, \vec{\omega}')(\vec{\omega}' \cdot \vec{n}) \, d\vec{\omega}' \,. \tag{9.2}$$

To evaluate this integral efficiently it is worth considering the properties of the BRDF, f_r, and the incoming radiance, L_i.

The BRDF is often a combination of two components: a smooth (diffuse) and a sharp (specular) component. This information is very useful when evaluating the BRDF, and we therefore split the BRDF into the sum of two terms: a specular/glossy term, $f_{r,S}$, and a diffuse term, $f_{r,D}$ (note that these do not have to be Lambertian $f_{r,d}$ or perfect specular $f_{r,s}$):

$$f_r(x, \vec{\omega}', \vec{\omega}) = f_{r,S}(x, \vec{\omega}', \vec{\omega}) + f_{r,D}(x, \vec{\omega}', \vec{\omega}) \,. \tag{9.3}$$

Similarly the incoming radiance is the sum of three components:

$$L_i(x, \vec{\omega}') = L_{i,l}(x, \vec{\omega}') + L_{i,c}(x, \vec{\omega}') + L_{i,d}(x, \vec{\omega}') \,, \tag{9.4}$$

where

- $L_{i,l}(x, \vec{\omega}')$ is direct illumination from the light sources.

- $L_{i,c}(x, \vec{\omega}')$ is caustics—indirect illumination from the light sources via specular reflection or transmission.

- $L_{i,d}(x, \vec{\omega}')$ is indirect illumination from the light sources that has been reflected diffusely at least once.

We can combine our classifications of the BRDF and the incoming radiance and split the expression for reflected radiance into a sum of four integrals:

$$
\begin{aligned}
L_r(x, \vec{\omega}) &= \int_\Omega f_r(x, \vec{\omega}', \vec{\omega}) L_i(x, \vec{\omega}')(\vec{\omega}' \cdot \vec{n}) \, d\vec{\omega}' \\
&= \int_\Omega f_r(x, \vec{\omega}', \vec{\omega}) L_{i,l}(x, \vec{\omega}')(\vec{\omega}' \cdot \vec{n}) \, d\vec{\omega}' + \\
&\quad \int_\Omega f_{r,S}(x, \vec{\omega}', \vec{\omega})(L_{i,c}(x, \vec{\omega}') + L_{i,d}(x, \vec{\omega}'))(\vec{\omega}' \cdot \vec{n}) \, d\vec{\omega}' + \\
&\quad \int_\Omega f_{r,D}(x, \vec{\omega}', \vec{\omega}) L_{i,c}(x, \vec{\omega}')(\vec{\omega}' \cdot \vec{n}) \, d\vec{\omega}' + \\
&\quad \int_\Omega f_{r,D}(x, \vec{\omega}', \vec{\omega}) L_{i,d}(x, \vec{\omega}')(\vec{\omega}' \cdot \vec{n}) \, d\vec{\omega}' .
\end{aligned}
\tag{9.5}
$$

This is the equation used whenever we need to compute the reflected radiance from a surface. In the following sections we discuss the evaluation of each of the integrals in the equation in more detail.

9.3   Pass 1: Photon Tracing

As shown in the previous section the incoming radiance is split into a sum of several components. In particular there is a caustics component and an indirect illumination component.

We have already seen how caustics are difficult to compute using standard Monte Carlo ray-tracing techniques, whereas the photon map is very efficient for caustics. For efficiency reasons it is therefore desirable to have a *caustics photon map* that only represents caustics. In addition we can use a *global photon map* to represent *all* illumination including caustics and direct illumination. It will become clear in the rendering section (Section 9.4) why this is useful.

9.3.1   The Caustics Photon Map

The caustics photon map contains photons that have been reflected or transmitted via one specular surface before hitting a diffuse surface. In the path notation these are LS+D.

Figure 9.1 illustrates the computation of the caustics photon map. Photons are emitted toward the glass sphere and stored as they hit the diffuse floor in the model. Once a caustic photon hits a diffuse material, it is terminated. Diffuse materials do not generate caustics.[1]

---

[1] For scenes with strong indirect illumination it may be useful to allow caustic photons to reflect diffusely also. This might make it possible to render caustics due to indirect illumination more efficiently. Here, these types of "caustics" are rendered using Monte Carlo ray tracing.

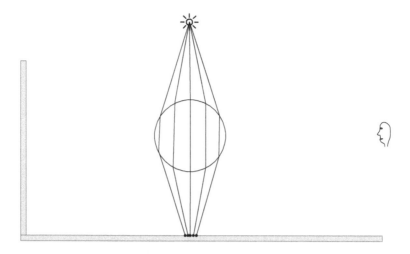

Figure 9.1. The caustics photon map is built by tracing photons only towards the specular surfaces in the model. All photons that are reflected or transmitted by a specular surface will be stored if they hit a diffuse surface. Once a photon hits a diffuse surface it is terminated.

The caustics photon map is used to render caustics that are seen directly by the eye, and it should therefore be of high quality. This means containing enough photons such that the amount of blur and other potential artifacts are reduced to an acceptable minimum. Fortunately, caustics are often focusing phenomena, in which case even very few photons can give good results.

To build the caustics photon map quickly it pays off to concentrate the emitted photons in the directions toward the specular surfaces. These can either be identified by the renderer, or for more control, explicitly (meaning that a person specifies exactly which objects generate caustics). For artistic control this concept can be extended such that the renderer only allows such objects to actually generate caustics. Similarly it may be useful to place constraints on which objects can receive a caustic. This would allow an animator to specify, for example, that a glass of cognac should create a caustic only on a table. This information gives more control to the animator, but it also makes it possible to make the renderer faster by computing only a limited number of caustics.

The projection map is particularly useful for computing caustics. It is often the case that a model contains a small object (such as a glass) that creates a caustic. The projection map makes it possible to concentrate the emitted photons towards this small object. This is better than using a sto-

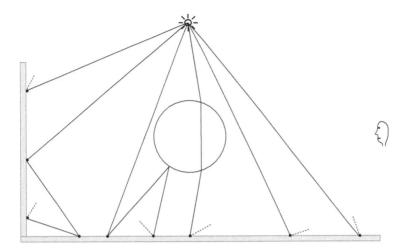

Figure 9.2. The global photon map is created by tracing photons towards all objects in the model. During photon tracing all surfaces can reflect and transmit photons. All photons that hit a diffuse surface are stored in the global photon map.

chastic approach, which might miss important caustic generators. Caustics in particular can be very intense even from small objects, and the projection map can give very good speedups while ensuring that these important caustics are simulated.

9.3.2   The Global Photon Map

The global photon map contains all photons that hit diffuse surfaces in the model. The photons in the global photon map represent direct illumination, indirect illumination, and caustics (in path notation: $L(S|D)*D$). This obviously means that we cannot just add the caustics photon map and the global photon map to get a full solution. The rendering step must be careful not to add terms twice.

The global photon map is built by tracing photons towards all objects in the model and storing these as they hit diffuse surfaces. Diffuse surfaces also reflect photons, unlike the caustics photon map. This is shown in Figure 9.2.

The ideas and optimizations that apply to the caustics photon map also work for the global photon map. The renderer does not have to identify specular surfaces, but it might still be useful to build in tools to allow a technical director to control which surfaces should generate indirect illumination and which surfaces should display indirect illumination. The

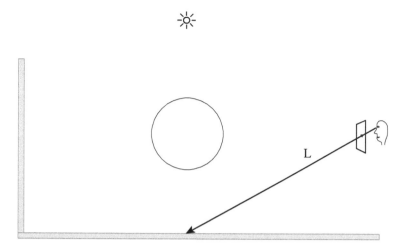

Figure 9.3. The radiance through a pixel is estimated by tracing a ray from the eye through the pixel and computing the reflected radiance at the first surface intersected by the ray.

projection map is still useful for the global photon map in order to concentrate emitted photons towards the geometry (for example, in a model where light sources are far away from the geometry).

9.4 Pass 2: Rendering

The final image is rendered using distribution ray tracing, in which the radiance of each pixel is evaluated by averaging a number of sample estimates. Each sample estimate is computed by tracing a ray from the eye through a pixel into the scene (see Figure 9.3). At the first surface intersected by the ray we evaluate Equation 9.5.

In the following it will be explained how each component of Equation 9.5 is computed. We distinguish between two different types of computations: an accurate and an approximate.

The accurate computation is used if the surface is seen directly by the eye or perhaps via a few specular reflections. It is also used if the distance between the ray origin and the intersection point is below a small threshold value—to eliminate potential inaccurate color bleeding effects in corners. The approximate evaluation is used if the ray intersecting the surface has been reflected diffusely since it left the eye or if the ray contributes little to the pixel radiance.

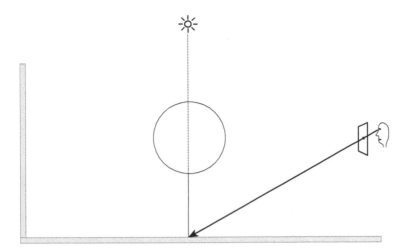

Figure 9.4. Direct illumination is evaluated accurately using ray tracing. A shadow ray is traced between the light source and the point of interest to determine if the point is illuminated or in shadow.

9.4.1 Direct Illumination

Direct illumination is given by the term

$$\int_{\Omega} f_r(x, \vec{\omega}', \vec{\omega}) L_{i,l}(x, \vec{\omega}')(\vec{\omega}' \cdot \vec{n}) \, d\vec{\omega}' , \tag{9.6}$$

and it represents the contribution to the reflected radiance due to direct illumination. This term is often the most important part of the reflected radiance and it has to be computed accurately, since it determines lighting effects to which the eye is highly sensitive, such as shadow edges.

The accurate computation of the direct illumination is quite simple in ray-tracing-based methods. At the point of interest, shadow rays are sent towards the light sources to test for possible occlusion by objects. This is illustrated in Figure 9.4. If a shadow ray does not hit an object, the contribution from the light source is included in the integral; otherwise it is neglected. For large area light sources, several shadow rays are used to properly integrate the contribution and correctly render penumbra regions. This strategy can, however, be very costly, since a large number of shadow rays is needed to properly integrate the direct illumination.

It is also possible to use an extension to the photon-mapping algorithm in which *shadow photons* are used to classify regions with full illumination, penumbra, and shadow [46]. Shadow photons are photons with negative power created by tracing photons from the light source through objects and storing them on diffuse surfaces. By examining the local distribution of shadow photons and photons coming directly from the light source, it is possible to quickly estimate the shadow properties of a given region. This approach can lead to considerable speedups in scenes with large area light sources that are normally very costly to render using standard ray tracing. The approach is stochastic though, so it might miss shadows from small objects in case these aren't intersected by any photons. This is a problem with all techniques that use stochastic evaluation of visibility. See Section 11.5 for more detail on the shadow photon approach.

The approximate evaluation of the direct illumination is the radiance estimate obtained from the global photon map (no shadow rays or light source evaluations are used!). This is seen in Figure 9.7 where the global photon map is used in the evaluation of the incoming light for the secondary diffuse reflection.

9.4.2   Specular and Glossy Reflection

Specular and glossy reflection is computed by evaluation of the term

$$\int_{\Omega} f_{r,S}(x, \vec{\omega}', \vec{\omega})(L_{i,c}(x, \vec{\omega}') + L_{i,d}(x, \vec{\omega}'))(\vec{\omega}' \cdot \vec{n}) \, d\vec{\omega}' \, . \tag{9.7}$$

The photon map is not used in the evaluation of this integral since it is strongly dominated by $f_{r,S}$, which has a narrow peak around the mirror direction. Using the photon map to optimize the integral would require a huge number of photons in order to make a useful classification of the different directions within the peak of $f_{r,S}$ (we have shown that this can be done in Figure 8.8). To save memory this strategy is not used, and the integral is evaluated using standard Monte Carlo ray tracing optimized with importance sampling based on $f_{r,S}$. This is still quite efficient for glossy surfaces and the integral can in most situations be computed using only a small number of sample rays. This is illustrated in Figure 9.5.

9.4.3   Caustics

Caustics are represented by the integral

$$\int_{\Omega} f_{r,D}(x, \vec{\omega}', \vec{\omega}) L_{i,c}(x, \vec{\omega}')(\vec{\omega}' \cdot \vec{n}) \, d\vec{\omega}' \, . \tag{9.8}$$

The evaluation of this term is dependent on whether an accurate or an approximate computation is required.

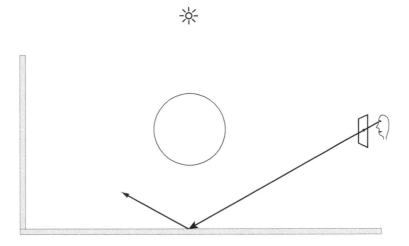

Figure 9.5. Specular and glossy reflections or transmissions are evaluated using recursive ray tracing. Ray tracing is good at integrating the contribution from the narrow peak in the BRDF. For glossy reflections it is possible to use a photon map, but this would require a large number of photons to get an accurate directional estimate.

For an accurate computation, the term is evaluated using a radiance estimate from the caustics photon map (see Figure 9.6). The number of photons in the caustics photon map is large, and we can expect good quality of the estimate. Caustics are never computed using Monte Carlo ray tracing, since this is a very inefficient method when it comes to rendering caustics.

The approximate evaluation of the caustics term is included in the radiance estimate from the global photon map.

9.4.4   Multiple Diffuse Reflections

The last term in Equation 9.5 is

$$\int_{\Omega} f_{r,D}(x, \vec{\omega}', \vec{\omega}) L_{i,d}(x, \vec{\omega}')(\vec{\omega}' \cdot \vec{n}) \, d\vec{\omega}' . \tag{9.9}$$

This term represents incoming light that has been reflected diffusely at least once since it left the light source. The light is then reflected diffusely by the surface (using $f_{r,D}$). Consequently the resulting illumination is very "soft".

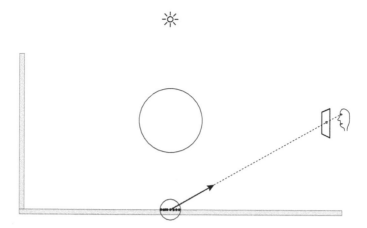

Figure 9.6. Caustics seen directly by the eye are rendered using the radiance estimate from the caustics photon map. No additional rays are traced.

The accurate evaluation of the integral is calculated using Monte Carlo ray tracing. Monte Carlo ray tracing is normally expensive for computing diffuse indirect illumination, but this integral has several properties that make it simpler. The indirect illumination is very smooth, since we have separated out caustics (computed using the caustics photon map). Caustics are often the main source for noise in Monte Carlo ray tracing. Furthermore, we can use information in the photon map about the incoming flux at x. This allows us to importance-sample not only according to the BRDF, but also according to the incoming lighting [41]. The details of this approach are described later in Chapter 11. Another very important optimization for Lambertian surfaces is the use of irradiance caching. Irradiance caching is a method that enables sparse evaluations of the irradiance by interpolating from previously cached values [118]. This method is also described in more detail in Chapter 11.

The approximate evaluation of indirect illumination is computed using the radiance estimate from the global photon map. Notice that this radiance estimate can be combined for caustics, direct illumination, and indirect illumination—this is the reason why the global photon map contains all the types of illumination. The computation of indirect diffuse illumination is illustrated in Figure 9.7.

9.5   Examples

The following pages contain several images and examples demonstrating the two-pass photon-mapping technique.

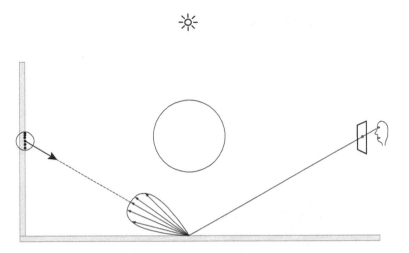

Figure 9.7. Indirect diffuse illumination is evaluated accurately by distribution ray tracing, where a number of sample rays are used to estimate the incoming light. For approximate evaluations (when these sample rays intersect another diffuse surface) the radiance estimate from the global photon map is used.

9.5.1 The Four Rendering Components

The four components (direct, specular, caustics, and indirect illumination) are shown in Figure 9.8 for the box scene (with a mirror ball to the left and a glass ball to the right). The sum of these four components (images) is the full global illumination solution shown in Figure 9.9.

For comparison the image in Figure 9.10 is a classic ray-tracing solution. Figure 9.11 includes soft shadows (distribution ray tracing), and Figure 9.12 includes caustics. Note that only the full global illumination solution in Figure 9.9 is capable of capturing the indirect illumination of the ceiling in the box.

9.5.2 Fractal Box

An example of a more complex scene is shown in Figure 9.13. The walls have been replaced with displacement-mapped surfaces (generated using a fractal midpoint subdivision algorithm) and the model contains more than 1.6 million elements. Notice that each wall segment is an instanced copy of the same fractal surface. With photon maps it is easy to take advantage of instancing, and the geometry does not have to be explicitly represented. We used 200,000 photons in the global photon map and 50,000

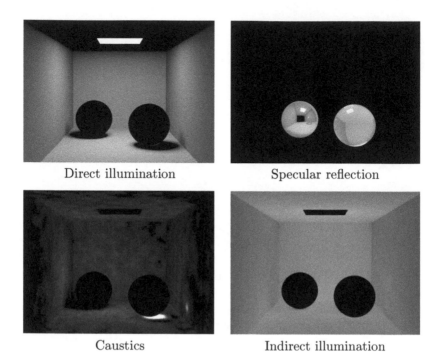

Direct illumination   Specular reflection

Caustics   Indirect illumination

Figure 9.8. The different components of the rendered solution.

in the caustics photon map. This is the same number of photons as in the simple box scene, and our reasoning for choosing the same values is that the complexity of the illumination is more or less the same as in the simple box scene. We want to capture the color bleeding from the colored walls and the indirect illumination of the ceiling. All in all we used the same parameters for the photon map as in the simple box model.

9.5.3   Box with Water

In the box scene in Figure 9.14 we have inserted a displacement-mapped water surface. To render this scene we used 500,000 photons in both the caustics and the global photon map, and up to 100 photons in the radiance estimate. We used a higher number of caustic photons due to the water surface, which causes the entire floor to be illuminated by the photons in the caustics photon map. Also the number of photons in the global photon map has been increased to account for the more complex indirect illumination in the scene. The water surface is made up of 20,000 triangles.

Figure 9.9. The box scene with full global illumination. (See Color Plate VII)

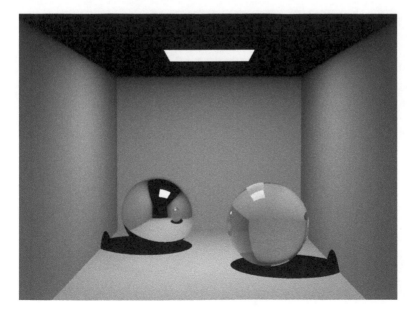

Figure 9.10. The box scene ray-traced. (See Color Plate VI.)

Figure 9.11. The box scene with soft shadows.

Figure 9.12. The box scene with caustics.

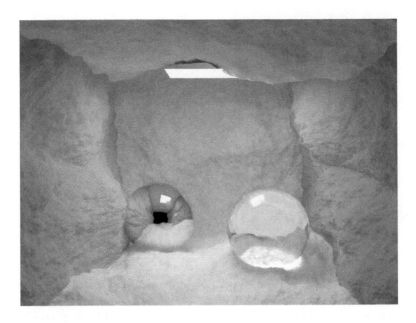

Figure 9.13. Fractal box.

Figure 9.14. Box with water.

Figure 9.15. Two bunnies represented using points. The shape of each bunny is represented using roughly 35,000 points. Using a technique for ray tracing points [84], we can compute global illumination and caustics for this model using photon mapping. Notice the caustic on the wood bunny—here the photons are stored on a point cloud.

9.5.4 Global Illumination on a Point Cloud

Figure 9.15 demonstrates a simulation of global illumination in a model with point-sampled geometry. Each bunny is represented using less than 35,000 points. Using a technique for ray tracing points (introduced in [84]) we can store photons on this geometry. This allows us to simulate caustics on the point-sampled wood bunny due to light focused through the point sampled glass bunny.

9.5.5 A Mountain Landscape

Figure 9.16 demonstrates a mountain landscape (Little Matterhorn) illuminated with sky and sunlight. To represent the illumination of the landscape, we used approximately 100,000 photons emitted both from the sun as well as the sky. The low number of photons compared with the high number of polygons (200 million) is possible due to the relatively simple illumination configuration.

12:30pm

6:30pm

Figure 9.16. A rendering of a geometric model of Little Matterhorn with trees (200 million polygons) in the middle of the day and at sunset. We used just 100,000 photons for this model to simulate the illumination from the sun as well as the sky. (See Color Plate VIII.)

9.5.6 The Courtyard House by Mies van der Rohe

Photon mapping makes it possible to simulate global illumination in complex models, such as the architectural model shown in Figure 9.17. The images are from an animation [49] that demonstrates how the natural lighting (skylight and sunlight) of a model changes during a day.

7am

8am

10am

3pm

6pm

7pm

Figure 9.17. A simulation of the lighting in the unbuilt "Courtyard House with Curved Elements" by Ludwig Mies van der Rohe. (See Color Plate X.)

10

Participating Media

In the previous chapters it was assumed that all photon interactions happen at surfaces. This is only the case in a vacuum. Even clean air scatters photons—this is the reason why the sky is blue. Often, we can ignore the presence of clean air in a model, but this is no longer the case for large (outdoor) models or when the air is filled with dust and other particles. Dusty air, clouds, and silty water are all examples of participating media, and the presence of these phenomena requires new light transport techniques.

Another class of participating media is translucent materials such as marble, skin, and plants. To perform a full simulation of the subsurface scattering inside such materials, it is necessary to solve the same basic equations as in the case of general participating media.

Photon mapping is very good at handling participating media, and it was the first method that demonstrated a full simulation of subsurface scattering in graphics [23, 50], and the first method to efficiently simulate volume caustics [48].

Before going into the details of how to use photon mapping in participating media this chapter begins by reviewing the light transport properties of participating media.

10.1   Light Scattering in Participating Media

When a photon enters a participating medium, it can either continue unaffected through the medium or it can interact with the medium at a given location. When a photon interacts with a medium one of two things can happen: it is either absorbed or scattered. The probability of a photon being either scattered or absorbed as it moves through a medium is given by the scattering coefficient, σ_s, and the absorption coefficient, σ_a. For a light ray moving through the medium, this can be seen as a continuous change in the radiance of the ray.

The change in radiance, L, in the direction, $\vec{\omega}$, due to out-scattering is given by the following equation:

$$(\vec{\omega} \cdot \nabla) L(x, \vec{\omega}) = -\sigma_s(x) L(x, \vec{\omega}) \ , \qquad (10.1)$$

and the change due to absorption is:

$$(\vec{\omega} \cdot \nabla) L(x, \vec{\omega}) = -\sigma_a(x) L(x, \vec{\omega}) \ . \qquad (10.2)$$

As it can be seen from these equations the radiance is reduced due to light being either scattered or absorbed. The combined loss in radiance is given by:

$$(\vec{\omega} \cdot \nabla) L(x, \vec{\omega}) = -\sigma_t(x) L(x, \vec{\omega}) \ , \qquad (10.3)$$

where $\sigma_t = \sigma_s + \sigma_a$ is the extinction coefficient.

As we move through the media there will also be a gain in radiance due to in-scattering of light. The change of radiance due to in-scattering is given by:

$$(\vec{\omega} \cdot \nabla) L(x, \vec{\omega}) = \sigma_s(x) \int_{\Omega_{4\pi}} p(x, \vec{\omega}', \vec{\omega}) L_i(x, \vec{\omega}') \, d\vec{\omega}' \ , \qquad (10.4)$$

where the incident radiance, L_i, is integrated over all directions on the sphere, $\Omega_{4\pi}$. $p(x, \vec{\omega}', \vec{\omega})$ is the phase function describing the distribution of the scattered light.

Finally, there can be a gain in radiance due to emission, L_e, from the medium (i.e., a flame), and it is given by:

$$(\vec{\omega} \cdot \nabla) L(x, \vec{\omega}) = \sigma_a(x) L_e(x, \vec{\omega}) \ . \qquad (10.5)$$

By combining Equations 10.3, 10.4, and 10.5 we find the total change in radiance per unit distance:

$$
\begin{aligned}
(\vec{\omega} \cdot \nabla) L(x, \vec{\omega}) \ = \ & \sigma_a(x) L_e(x, \vec{\omega}) - \sigma_t(x) L(x, \vec{\omega}) \ + \\
& \sigma_s(x) \int_{\Omega_{4\pi}} p(x, \vec{\omega}', \vec{\omega}) L_i(x, \vec{\omega}') \, d\vec{\omega}' .
\end{aligned}
\qquad (10.6)
$$

10.2   The Volume Rendering Equation

By integrating Equation 10.6 on both sides for a segment of length s, and adding the contribution of incoming radiance from the other side of the medium we find that:

$$
\begin{aligned}
L(x, \vec{\omega}) \;=\; & \int_0^s e^{-\tau(x, x')} \sigma_a(x') L_e(x', \vec{\omega})\, dx' \\
& + \int_0^s e^{-\tau(x, x')} \sigma_s(x') \int_{\Omega_{4\pi}} p(x', \vec{\omega}', \vec{\omega}) L_i(x', \vec{\omega}')\, d\vec{\omega}'\, dx' \\
& + e^{-\tau(x, x+s\vec{\omega})} L(x - s\vec{\omega}, \vec{\omega})
\end{aligned}
\tag{10.7}
$$

where the optical depth $\tau(x, x')$ is given by:

$$
\tau(x, x') = \int_x^{x'} \sigma_t(t)\, dt \; .
\tag{10.8}
$$

Equation 10.7 is the *volume rendering equation*, and it is the equation that must be solved in order to render participating media. The equation is more complex than the rendering equation. It is describing radiance in a five-dimensional space compared with the four-dimensional space (surface and direction) for the rendering equation (Section 2.5). This is due to the fact that light is influenced by light at every point in space, not just the points on other surfaces. This is one of the reasons why participating media is costly to simulate.

10.3   The Phase Function

The phase function describes the distribution of the scattered light in participating media. Unlike the BRDF for surfaces, the phase function must integrate to one over the sphere:

$$
\int_{\Omega_{4\pi}} p(x, \vec{\omega}', \vec{\omega})\, d\vec{\omega}' = 1 \; .
\tag{10.9}
$$

Even though it seems similar to the BRDF used for surfaces, there are two important differences: the phase function is unitless and normalized (the amount of scattering and absorption is controlled by the scattering and absorption coefficients).

The phase function often depends only on the angle, θ, between the incoming ray and the scattered ray, and it can be written as $p(\theta)$ where $\theta = 0$ is the forward direction and $\theta = \pi$ is the backward direction. To specify the preferred scattering direction of the phase function (forward or backward) one can compute the average cosine of the scattered direction, g, as:

$$g(x) = \int_{\Omega_{4\pi}} p(x, \vec{\omega}', \vec{\omega}) \cos\theta' d\vec{\omega}' . \tag{10.10}$$

The value of $g \in [-1, 1]$ will be positive for forward scattering and negative for backward scattering. It is also the parameter for the commonly used Henyey-Greenstein phase function (described later).

The shape of the phase function is also used to classify the participating medium. The scattering is either isotropic or anisotropic. That is, any phase function with a preferential scattering direction is anisotropic (this is the most common case); otherwise the scattering is isotropic. If the phase function further depends on the orientation of the medium, then the medium is anisotropic; otherwise it is isotropic. Notice that, unlike surfaces, we have two components that are either isotropic or anisotropic.

10.3.1   Isotropic Scattering

The phase function for isotropic scattering is a constant:

$$p(\theta) = \frac{1}{4\pi} . \tag{10.11}$$

This means that a photon that is scattered will be scattered in any random direction without a history where it came from (Figure 10.1 (a)).

10.3.2   The Henyey-Greenstein Phase Function

The most commonly used phase function is the empirical Henyey-Greenstein phase function [35]. It was introduced to explain scattering by intergalactic dust, but it has since been used to describe scattering in oceans, clouds, skin, stone, and more.

The function is:

$$p(\theta) = \frac{1 - g^2}{4\pi(1 + g^2 - 2g\cos\theta)^{1.5}} , \tag{10.12}$$

where $g \in] -1, 1[$ is an asymmetry parameter equal to the average cosine of the scattered directions (see Equation 10.10). Positive g gives forward scattering and negative g gives backward scattering ($g = 0$ is isotropic scattering). Higher values of g makes the scattering more preferential ($g = 1$ gives pure forward scattering in the same direction). This is illustrated in

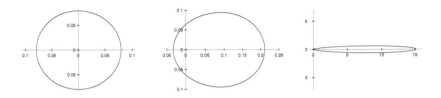

Figure 10.1. The Henyey-Greenstein phase function with different g. From left to right $g = 0.0$, $g = 0.3$, and $g = 0.9$.

Figure 10.1. The function is essentially giving ellipsoid-shaped scattering distributions where the shape of the ellipsoid is controlled by g.

For more complex types of scattering one can use a combination of several Henyey-Greenstein functions.

$$p(\theta) = \sum_{i=1}^{N} w_i \frac{1 - g_i^2}{4\pi(1 + g_i^2 - 2g_i \cos\theta)^{1.5}} \quad \text{where} \quad \sum_{i=1}^{N} w_i = 1 \quad (10.13)$$

Here g_i controls the shape of each lobe and w_i the weight. Such a multi-lobed function can be used to model more complex scattering, and it can give very realistic results. Commonly used is a sum of a forward scattering and a backward scattering lobe.

Another advantage of the Henyey-Greenstein function is that it can be importance-sampled very easily. Given the incoming direction, $\vec{\omega}$, of a photon, the angle, θ, of the new scattered direction is given by:

$$\cos\theta = \frac{1}{2g}\left(1 + g^2 - \left(\frac{1 - g^2}{1 - g + 2g\xi}\right)^2\right), \quad (10.14)$$

where ξ is a uniform random number between zero and one. θ is the same angle as in the phase function. The rotation ϕ is uniformly distributed.

10.3.3 The Schlick Phase Function

For most applications the accurate shape of the empirical Henyey-Greenstein phase function is less important. Since the shape of the function is close to an ellipsoid, one might approximate it by an ellipsoid and thereby eliminate the relatively costly 1.5 exponent in the denominator. This observation was made by Schlick [9] who used the following phase function:

$$p(\theta) = \frac{1 - k^2}{4\pi(1 + k \cos\theta)^2}, \quad (10.15)$$

where $k \in \,]-1, 1[$ is used to control the preferred direction of the scattering (similar to g in the Henyey-Greenstein function). $k = 0$ gives isotropic scattering, $k > 0$ is forward scattering, and $k < 0$ is backward scattering.

The Schlick phase function is also very simple to importance-sample. The angle, θ, of the new scattered direction is given by:

$$\cos \theta = \frac{2\xi + k - 1}{2k\xi - k + 1} \, , \tag{10.16}$$

where ξ is a uniformly distributed random number between zero and one. The rotation is uniformly distributed.

10.3.4   Other Phase Functions

There are many other phase functions available to describe scattering of light. In particular a number of analytical phase functions have been derived for the scattering of electromagnetic waves from special geometries.

The type of geometry most frequently used is homogeneous spheres. This makes the medium isotropic, and the scattering can be explained with a phase function that takes only the scattered angle as a parameter. Phase functions have been derived for the case when the medium contains many small spheres that each reflect light diffusely according to Lambert's law. More interesting phase functions have been derived for dielectric and metallic spherical particles.

Scattering from very small spheres (smaller than the wavelength of light) is explained by Rayleigh scattering [11]. The phase function is almost uniform, but the scattering coefficient includes a dependency on the wavelength raised to the fourth power. This makes the scattering highly wavelength-dependent, with blue light being scattered much more than the other components of the light. Rayleigh scattering can be used to model scattering of light from molecules in the atmosphere, and to model the blue sky and red sunsets.

For homogeneous spheres of arbitrary size the scattering pattern becomes more complex. It is necessary to use Mie theory [65] to compute the phase function. These formulas are quite complex and difficult to use, and it makes sense to use them only when accurate scattering of homogeneous spheres is needed. An interesting observation is that Mie scattering often is characterized by a strong forward scattering component and a smaller backward scattering component. This scattering pattern can, for most graphics simulations, be adequately modeled with a multi-lobed Henyey-Greenstein phase function.

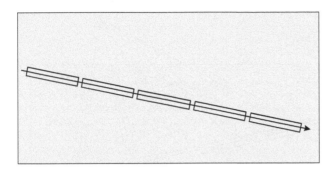

Figure 10.2. The ray-marching algorithm computes the contribution from the medium by dividing the ray into smaller segments. For each segment the medium is assumed to be homogeneous.

10.4 Ray Marching

The volume rendering equation (Equation 10.7) can, except for the simplest cases, only be solved by using numerical integration. A numerical integration can be done by taking small steps through the medium and making some local simplifying assumptions within the segment considered. This approach is called ray marching.

In ray marching the ray is divided into little segments of length Δx. For each segment it is assumed that the incoming light is constant and that the properties of the medium are constant. With these simplifications the radiance from a small segment due to direct illumination can be computed as:

$$L(x,\vec{\omega}) = \sum_{l}^{N} L_l(x,\vec{\omega}_l')p(x,\vec{\omega}_l',\vec{\omega})\sigma_s(x)\Delta x \ + \ e^{-\sigma_t\Delta x}L(x+\vec{\omega}\Delta x,\vec{\omega}) \ ,$$

(10.17)

where N is the number of light sources in the scene, and L_l is the radiance from each light source. The first term sums the contribution from the segment due to direct illumination and the last term is the radiance entering the segment at the backside.

For a medium of a finite size, ray marching can be used to compute the radiance due to direct illumination (single scattering) by recursively calling the formula to move backwards through the medium (see Figure 10.2).

$$L_{n+1}(x,\vec{\omega}) = \sum_{l}^{N} L_l(x,\vec{\omega}_l')p(x,\vec{\omega}_l',\vec{\omega})\sigma_s(x)\Delta x \ + \ e^{-\sigma_t\Delta x}L_n(x+\vec{\omega}\Delta x,\vec{\omega}) \ .$$

(10.18)

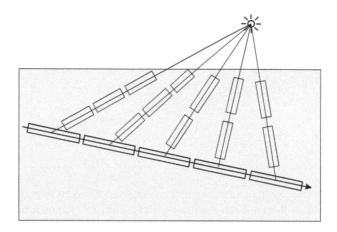

Figure 10.3. The contribution from the light source must be attenuated based on the medium along the shadow ray. In non-homogeneous media this requires a ray-marching integration for each shadow ray.

Notice that the direct illumination must be attenuated properly based on the distance that the shadow ray moves through the medium (for non-homogeneous media it is often necessary to integrate this using another ray-marching evaluation). This is shown in Figure 10.3.

To improve visual appearance and reduce aliasing artifacts it is often useful to randomly pick the sample position at which the direct illumination is computed. This can be done either locally within each segment, or globally by adding a small random offset to the entry point of the ray.

Equation 10.18 includes only single scattering. For a multiple scattering simulation, it is necessary to integrate all of the in-scattered radiance at every segment. This can be done by sampling the sphere of directions around the segment (point) of interest, which leads to the following formulation:

$$L_{n+1}(x,\vec{\omega}) = \sum_l^N L_l(x,\vec{\omega}_l')p(x,\vec{\omega}_l',\vec{\omega})\sigma_s(x)\Delta x$$
$$+ \left\{ \frac{1}{S} \sum_{s=1}^{S} L_s(x,\vec{\omega}_s)p(x,\vec{\omega}_s',\vec{\omega}) \right\} \sigma_s(x)\Delta x$$
$$+ e^{-\sigma_t(x)\Delta x}L_n(x+\vec{\omega}\Delta x,\vec{\omega}). \qquad (10.19)$$

Here S sample rays are used to estimate the in-scattered light. The contribution from each sample ray is found by recursively evaluating this formula (which is already recursive!). As such this formula is very costly to evaluate, and one of the reasons why most simulations of participating media have excluded multiple scattering. In many cases, however, multiple scattering is essential to get the correct appearance. For example, a cloud will look very flat and dark grey without multiple scattering. In general it is necessary to simulate multiple scattering in media with a high albedo (i.e., scattering dominates over absorption). Fortunately, the photon map provides an efficient solution to this problem.

10.4.1 Adaptive Ray Marching

The ray marcher in Equation 10.19 is based on a uniform step size through the medium. For non-homogeneous media and media with local variations in the lighting (such as shadows), it is better to use adaptive ray marching. Adaptive ray marching uses segments of varying length to capture local changes more efficiently. This is usually done by adjusting the step size on the fly, based on the observed illumination and scattering properties. If a contrast in the illumination is seen or if the scattering properties (albedo or extinction coefficient) changes significantly in one step, then the segment can be subdivided into a sequence of smaller segments. The simplest method for doing this is a recursive ray marcher, where the midpoint of the segment is sampled recursively until the length of the segment is below a certain threshold, or until the contrast between the endpoints of the segment is sufficiently low.

Another simple method for non-homogeneous media is to adjust the step size based on the observed extinction coefficient. For media with unknown properties this can be very efficient. One possibility is to use a random step size computed as:

$$\Delta x = -\frac{\log \xi}{\sigma_t(x)} \, , \tag{10.20}$$

where $\xi \in]0 : 1[$ is a uniform random number. In this way the average step size will be the same as the average distance that a photon moves through the medium before an interaction.

10.5 Photon Tracing

When tracing photons in a scene with participating media, the photons interact with the media and are scattered and/or absorbed. If a photon hits a surface we use the techniques described in Chapter 5, and the photon is either absorbed, reflected, or transmitted. When a photon *enters* a participating medium, it does not scatter at the boundary of the medium. Instead

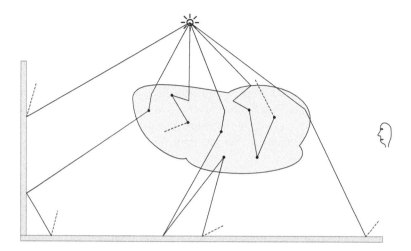

Figure 10.4. Photon tracing in a scene with a participating medium. The photons that enter the medium can be either scattered or absorbed. These photons are stored at the location of the interaction in a separate volume photon map. Photons that hit surfaces are scattered using the standard techniques for surfaces.

it moves through the medium until it is either scattered or absorbed. The probability that such an interaction happens is determined from the extinction coefficient. The average distance, d, that a photon moves through a medium before the next interaction is given by:

$$d = \frac{1}{\sigma_t} \, . \tag{10.21}$$

A beam of light passing through a medium will have its intensity reduced by $e^{-\sigma_t s}$ where s is the distance through the medium. For nonhomogeneous media σ_t is replaced by $\tau(0, d)$, which is then evaluated using ray marching. When tracing photons, we can importance-sample according to this formula by using the following expression for the distance, d, to the next interaction:

$$d = -\frac{\log \xi}{\sigma_t} \, , \tag{10.22}$$

where $\xi \in]0, 1]$ is a uniformly distributed random number. If we use this formula to determine the distance to the next event, then we do not have to reduce the power of the photon as it moves through the medium.

10.5.1 Photon Scattering

At the point of interaction the photon is either absorbed or scattered. The probability of scattering is given by the scattering albedo, Λ:

$$\Lambda = \frac{\sigma_s}{\sigma_t} . \tag{10.23}$$

Based on the value of Λ, a new scattered photon can be generated by scaling the power of the incoming photon with Λ. This approach will work, but it will in many cases lead to a large number of photons in the media with a very low power. This is wasteful. A better approach is to use Russian roulette to decide whether the photon is scattered or absorbed. This is done by comparing a random number $\xi \in [0,1]$ to Λ:

$$\text{Given } \xi \in [0,1] \rightarrow \left\{ \begin{array}{ll} \xi \leq \Lambda & \text{Photon is scattered} \\ \xi > \Lambda & \text{Photon is absorbed} \end{array} \right. \tag{10.24}$$

If the photon is scattered it will continue with the same power (no scaling by Λ is necessary). For colored photons it may be necessary to use an average albedo, and then scale the individual components of the scattered photon (similar to the use of Russian roulette for surfaces).

The direction of a scattered photon should be computed by importance-sampling the phase function. The phase functions for participating media are often highly anisotropic, and a uniform sampling is therefore very inefficient. It is much better to use the importance-sampling formulas presented in Section 10.3.

10.5.2 Photon Storing

When a photon interacts with a medium it is stored (independent of whether the event is scattering or absorption). For participating media we use a separate *volume photon map*. This is due to the fact that the radiance estimate in a participating media is different than the estimate for surfaces (see Section 10.6).

A useful optimization for participating media is to store only photons that have been scattered at least once before (as shown in Figure 10.4). In this way the contribution due to direct illumination is omitted—this component can be computed very easily using traditional techniques. See Section 10.7 for more detail.

10.5.3 Photon Emission

Photons can also be emitted from the participating media. An accurate model of a candle flame might simulate the motion and temperature of the hot gas, and, based on these parameters, photons can be emitted from locations in the media with a spectrum based on the local conditions. This would be more accurate than approaches that try to approximate the flame with a point light source.

10.6   The Volume Radiance Estimate

How can we estimate the out-scattered radiance at a given point inside the medium, based on the stored photons? The two-dimensional approximation for surfaces cannot be used. To compute the out-scattered radiance, L_o, we need to evaluate Equation 10.4:

$$(\vec{\omega} \cdot \nabla) L_o(x, \vec{\omega}) = \sigma_s(x) \int_{\Omega_{4\pi}} p(x, \vec{\omega}', \vec{\omega}) \, L(x, \vec{\omega}') \, d\vec{\omega}' \, . \qquad (10.25)$$

The stored photons represent incoming flux, so this equation should be converted to an integral over incoming flux. This is done using the relationship between flux and radiance in a participating medium:

$$L(x, \vec{\omega}) = \frac{d^2 \Phi(x, \vec{\omega})}{\sigma_s(x) \, d\vec{\omega} \, dV} \qquad (10.26)$$

Combining Equations 10.25 and 10.26 we get [48]:

$$
\begin{aligned}
(\vec{\omega} \cdot \nabla) L_o(x, \vec{\omega}) &= \sigma_s(x) \int_{\Omega_{4\pi}} p(x, \vec{\omega}', \vec{\omega}) \frac{d^2 \Phi(x, \vec{\omega})}{\sigma_s(x) \, d\vec{\omega} \, dV} \, d\vec{\omega} \\
&= \int_{\Omega_{4\pi}} p(x, \vec{\omega}', \vec{\omega}) \frac{d^2 \Phi(x, \vec{\omega})}{dV} .
\end{aligned}
\qquad (10.27)
$$

Notice the similarity with the surface radiance estimate (Equation 7.6). Again we have an equation where we need to estimate the local photon density. However, for participating media, the density should be measured over the entire volume instead of just a surface.

Using the same strategy as for the surface radiance estimate we can locate the n nearest photons, and using the same assumptions for the estimate we get:

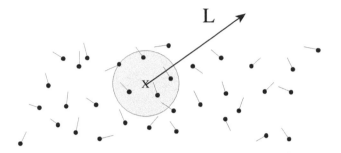

Figure 10.5. Out-scattered radiance is evaluated by locating the nearest photons in the volume photon map in order to estimate the local photon density. This approach can be seen as expanding a sphere around the intersection point until it contains enough photons. The photon density is estimated based on the volume of the sphere.

$$
\begin{aligned}
(\vec{\omega} \cdot \nabla) L_o(x, \vec{\omega}) &= \int_{\Omega_{4\pi}} p(x, \vec{\omega}', \vec{\omega}) \frac{d^2 \Phi(x, \vec{\omega})}{dV} \\
&\approx \sum_{p=1}^{n} p(x, \vec{\omega}'_p, \vec{\omega}) \frac{\Delta \Phi_p(x, \vec{\omega}'_p)}{\Delta V} \\
&\approx \sum_{p=1}^{n} p(x, \vec{\omega}'_p, \vec{\omega}) \frac{\Delta \Phi_p(x, \vec{\omega}'_p)}{\frac{4}{3}\pi r^3} .
\end{aligned}
\tag{10.28}
$$

Here we have substituted the small volume ΔV with the volume of the sphere ($\frac{4}{3}\pi r^3$) containing all the photons. Similar to the surface estimate, this can be seen as expanding a sphere around the intersection point until it contains the n nearest photons. The volume of the sphere determines the density of the photons. This is shown in Figure 10.5.

10.7 Rendering Participating Media

With the volume photon map and the ability to compute a radiance estimate, we have the tools necessary to render scenes with participating media. The rendering technique is an extension of the two-pass algorithm presented in Chapter 9: the first pass is emitting photons from the light sources and storing them as they hit the surfaces or the media in the model; the second pass uses ray tracing to render the image. If a ray hits a surface, we use the approach described in Chapter 9. If the ray enters a participating medium, we use ray marching to integrate the illumination. We split

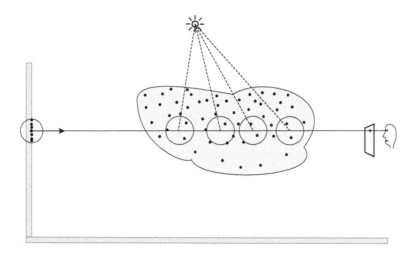

Figure 10.6. Participating media is rendered using ray marching. When a ray enters the medium, a ray-marching algorithm integrates the contribution from multiple scattering and direct illumination (single scattering). Multiple scattering is computed using the volume photon map and direct illumination is computed using ray tracing. If the ray hits a surface, we use the techniques described in Chapter 9.

the in-scattered radiance into single scattering, L_s, and multiple scattering, L_m:

$$L(x,\vec{\omega}) = L_s(x,\vec{\omega}) + L_m(x,\vec{\omega}) \ . \tag{10.29}$$

The single scattering term is evaluated using ray tracing, and the multiple scattering term is computed using the volume radiance estimate. This is shown in Figure 10.6.

By inserting the volume radiance estimate in the ray-marching algorithm (Equation 10.19) we get:

$$\begin{aligned}
L_{n+1}(x,\vec{\omega}) \ = \ & \sum_{l}^{N} L_l(x,\vec{\omega}_l')p(x,\vec{\omega}_l',\vec{\omega})\sigma_s(x)\Delta x \\
& + \left\{ \sum_{p=1}^{n} p(x,\vec{\omega}_p',\vec{\omega}) \frac{\Delta\Phi_p(x,\vec{\omega}_p')}{\frac{4}{3}\pi r^3} \right\} \Delta x \\
& + e^{-\sigma_t(x)\Delta x} L_n(x+\Delta x,\vec{\omega}) \ . \tag{10.30}
\end{aligned}$$

This is the equation used to integrate the contribution from participating media.

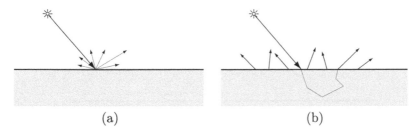

Figure 10.7. Traditional surface-based reflection shown in (a); subsurface scattering shown in (b).

10.8   Subsurface Scattering

Subsurface scattering happens in all non-metallic materials. In computer graphics it is often approximated by a diffuse reflection term where the assumption is that light entering the material leaves the material at the same location in a random direction (shown in Figure 10.7 (a)). For translucent materials such as marble, skin, and milk, this is a bad approximation. Translucent materials often have a soft appearance and light will bleed through thin slabs of the material. An example is a piece of paper illuminated from behind.

To accurately render translucent materials it is necessary to take into account the fact that light entering a material can leave the material at a different location, as shown in Figure 10.7 (b). The first method that fully simulated this phenomena was based on photon mapping and presented in [23, 50]. It uses the photon-mapping algorithm for participating media with some improvements specific to subsurface scattering.

10.8.1   Photon Tracing

To simulate subsurface scattering with photon mapping, we first build a photon map using photon tracing as shown in Figure 10.8. Here the photons are refracted at the material interface and traced through the material medium using the same techniques described earlier in this chapter. Each time a photon interacts with the material it is stored in the volume photon map. We exclude photons coming directly from the light source, as is the case for participating media since this contribution can be computed (with some approximations) using standard ray-tracing techniques.

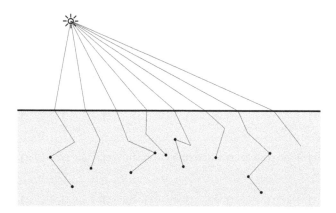

Figure 10.8. Photon tracing for subsurface scattering.

10.8.2 Rendering

Rendering of materials with subsurface scattering proceeds in a similar way as rendering of participating media. When a ray intersects a subsurface scattering material, it is refracted into the medium. Ray marching is used to evaluate the contribution from the medium along the refracted ray. For efficiency reasons the step size for the ray marcher is varied locally, based on the extinction coefficient. A good value is $\Delta x(x) = -\log \xi / \sigma_t(x)$, where $\xi \in]0, 1[$ is a uniform random number. For dense materials this ensures a small step size. Furthermore, the ray marcher should be stopped using Russian roulette sampling once the optical depth reaches a certain value.

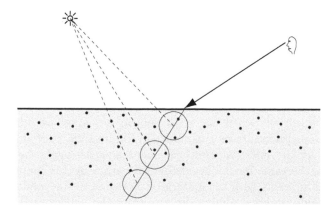

Figure 10.9. Rendering materials with subsurface scattering using the photon map.

The contribution due to in-scattered radiance is computed as a sum of two terms: a direct single-scattering term and a indirect multiple-scattering term. The indirect multiple-scattering term is computed using the volume radiance estimate described earlier, and the direct illumination is computed using ray tracing. The ray-tracing technique traces a shadow ray to the light source to check for visibility. This shadow ray goes straight through the material boundary; this is an approximation since the shadow ray should be refracted, but the configuration for the refraction is difficult to compute exactly. The only way to avoid this approximation is to use the photon map for all types of illumination. We can make the computation of direct illumination more accurate by estimating the true distance that the refracted ray would have moved through the medium:

$$d_i' = d_i \frac{|\vec{\omega} \cdot \vec{n}|}{\sqrt{1 - \left(\frac{1}{\eta}\right)^2 (1 - |\vec{\omega} \cdot \vec{n}|^2)}} . \tag{10.31}$$

Here d_i is the observed distance and d_i' is the estimate of the true distance; $\vec{n}$ is the normal at the surface location intersected by the shadow ray. The attenuation of the light from the light source should be modified using this equation.

10.9   Examples

The following pages contains several examples illustrating the simulation of participating media and subsurface scattering with photon mapping.

10.9.1   Rising Smoke

Figure 10.10 shows a multiple-scattering simulation in turbulent smoke. The smoke simulation is due to techniques described in Fedkiw et al. [25]. To render the smoke we used roughly two million photons. Multiple scattering is important for the realism of the smoke. A single-scattering simulation looks flat in comparison.

10.9.2   Smoke Flowing Past a Sphere

Figure 10.11 is another smoke simulation from [25]. It illustrates a multiple-scattering simulation for an animation showing smoke flowing past a sphere. Roughly 1–2 million photons were used per frame in this animation.

Figure 10.10. A simulation of multiple scattering in turbulent smoke rising due to buoyancy (from [25]).

10.9.3   A Volume Caustic

Figure 10.12 shows a volume caustic. The volume caustic is a result of light being focused through the glass sphere and illuminating the fog medium. Here the volume caustic is simulated using 1,500,000 photons. For this simulation the adaptive ray-marching algorithm significantly reduces the rendering time by concentrating the effort on the focused beam rather than the other less interesting parts of the smoke.

10.9.4   Michelangelo's David

Figure 10.13 shows a rendering of Michelangelo's David (from [61]). The model has approximately 8 million triangles. We used one million photons to capture the multiple scattering component of the subsurface scattering simulation.

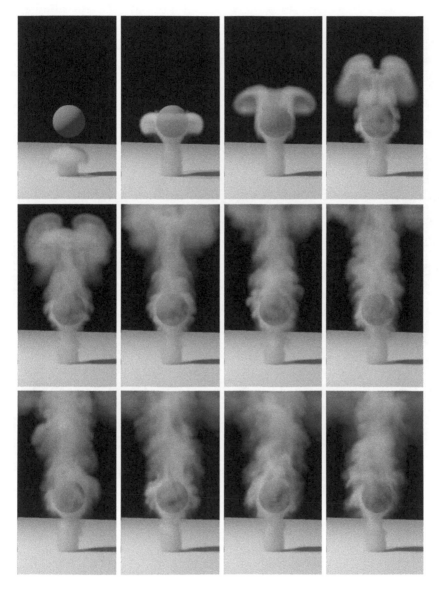

Figure 10.11. Sequence of rendered images from a simulation of smoke flowing past a sphere (from [25]). (See Color Plate IX.)

Figure 10.12. A volume caustic created as light focused through a glass ball illuminates the fog medium.

Figure 10.13. The David represented using approximately 8 million triangles. This image was rendered with subsurface scattering using photon mapping with roughly one million photons.

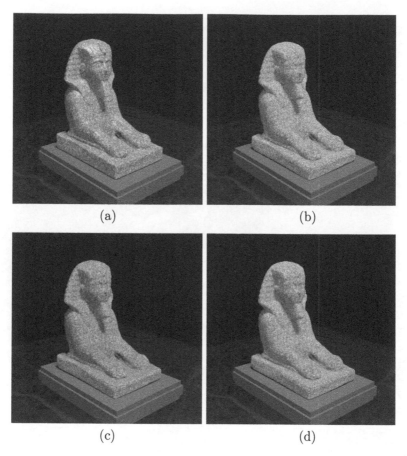

Figure 10.14. A weathering simulation of a granite sphinx from [23]. (a) is the fresh granite, (b) shows erosion due to salt, (c) shows reddening due to dissolved iron, and (d) shows the combined weathering effect due to salt and iron. (See Color Plate XI.)

10.9.5 A Weathered Granite Sphinx

The four images in Figure 10.14 demonstrate how photon mapping and subsurface scattering can render the result of a complex weathering simulation [23]. Subsurface scattering is the only way to correctly render the effect of weathering, which is due to changes in the material structure. Dissolved iron, in particular, is often present below the surface. Even without the weathering simulation the simulation of subsurface scattering is important for the overall appearance of granite.

Figure 10.15. A marble bust. Subsurface scattering is essential to capture the soft appearance of marble.

10.9.6 A Translucent Marble Bust

Marble is a translucent material and subsurface scattering is essential to capture the appearance of marble. Figure 10.15 is a simulation of a marble bust. Only 200,000 photons were used in this simulation. Subsurface scattering is important for the smooth appearance of marble, but it is also critical for correctly simulating translucency. This is particularly notice-able in Figure 10.16, which shows a close-up of the marble statue now illuminated from behind. Note how the light bleeds through the hair and

Figure 10.16. A translucent marble bust. (See Color Plate XII.)

the nose and still gives a soft appearance of the marble. Compare this with
the diffuse rendering of the same model and the same lighting conditions
in Figure 10.17. The diffuse rendering lacks the smooth and soft appearance and looks very hard and unattractive compared with the subsurface
scattering simulation.

Figure 10.17. A diffuse rendering of the marble bust. Notice the substantial difference with the full subsurface scattering simulation. The diffuse approximation gives the impression of a hard material. (See Color Plate XIII.)

11

Optimization Strategies

This chapter contains several different techniques for making a photon-mapping implementation faster and more efficient. Some of these ideas are fairly general, some are very important (such as irradiance caching), and some are special tricks for the photon map.

11.1 Irradiance Caching

The irradiance caching idea was introduced by Ward et al. in 1988 [118] as a method for speeding up the computation of indirect illumination (color bleeding) in a Monte Carlo ray tracer (Radiance [116]). It is a method for caching and re-using (via interpolation) irradiance values on Lambertian surfaces. As mentioned in Chapter 9 it can (and should!) be used in the rendering step of the two-pass photon-mapping algorithm to cache irradiance values at Lambertian surfaces.

Indirect illumination on diffuse surfaces is often the most costly component to compute in a Monte Carlo ray tracer, since it requires a large number of sample rays. This is the case even in the two-pass photon-mapping algorithm where only the first bounce of diffuse illumination is computed. Speeding up this computation is very important.

The irradiance at a location, x, on a diffuse surface is computed by sampling the incident radiance above x. This is equivalent to evaluating the integral in Equation 2.18. Instead of sampling the hemisphere uniformly, we can include the cosine from the diffuse BRDF, which gives the following equation for sampling the irradiance:

$$E(x) = \frac{\pi}{MN} \sum_{j=1}^{M} \sum_{i=1}^{N} L_{i,j}(\theta_j, \phi_i) , \qquad (11.1)$$

where

$$\theta_j = \sin^{-1}\left(\sqrt{\frac{j - \xi_1}{M}}\right) \quad \text{and} \quad \phi_i = 2\pi\frac{i - \xi_2}{N} . \qquad (11.2)$$

Here $\xi_1 \in [0,1]$ and $\xi_2 \in [0,1]$ are uniformly distributed random numbers, and M and N are the subdivision of the hemisphere. Note that we could have used $\theta_j = \sin^{-1}(\sqrt{\xi_1})$ and $\phi_i = 2\pi\xi_2$ instead; however, the formulation in Equation 11.2 includes a stratification of the hemisphere, which gives much better results than a naive random sampling.

The evaluation of Equation 11.1 requires tracing $M*N$ rays to estimate the incident radiance from different directions. To get good estimates it is usually necessary to use $M * N = 200$–5000 sample rays. This is very costly. An important observation made by Ward et al. [118] is that indirect illumination on diffuse surfaces often changes slowly in a model. As such it seems like a natural candidate for interpolation. The idea is to compute irradiance only at selected locations on the surfaces in the model and then interpolate irradiance for the remaining locations.

The decision whether to interpolate or compute irradiance at a location is based on the previously computed values. If we want to compute a new irradiance value at x we first look at the previously computed irradiance values. For each of those values we compute a weight, w_i, that tells us if we can use the value for interpolation.

For an irradiance value at x_i the weight is computed as:

$$w_i(x, \vec{n}) = \frac{1}{\epsilon_i(x, \vec{n})} , \qquad (11.3)$$

where $\epsilon_i(x)$ is an estimate of the amount of change in the irradiance from x_i to x. This change is estimated based on a split-sphere model [118]. This model assumes a hemisphere above x_i which is black on one half of the hemisphere and white on the other half. This type of hemisphere represents a sharp boundary in the incident illumination, and it can provide a good estimate of the worst change in the irradiance that we can observe as we move away from x_i. The two possible changes are: a change to the surface location and a change in the surface orientation (the normal). From this model the change in irradiance can be estimated as [118]:

$$\epsilon_i(x, \vec{n}) = E_i(x_i) \left\{ \frac{4}{\pi} \frac{\|x_i - x\|}{R_0} + \sqrt{2 - 2\vec{n} \cdot \vec{n}_i} \right\} , \qquad (11.4)$$

where $\vec{n}_i$ is the surface normal at x_i. E_i is the irradiance at x_i and R_0 is the harmonic mean distance to the objects seen from x_i. This value is computed as the reciprocal of the sum of reciprocal distances recorded for each ray when evaluating Equation 11.1.

For the weight w_i, we can use a slightly simplified version of Equation 11.4 and we find that:

$$w_i = \frac{1}{\frac{\|x_i - x\|}{R_0} + \sqrt{1 - 1\vec{n} \cdot \vec{n}_i}} . \qquad (11.5)$$

The value of this weight is an indication of how good an estimate the irradiance E_i is of the irradiance at x. The higher the weight the better the estimate. If it is too low then we cannot use it. Ward suggested only using weights where:

$$w_i(x, \vec{n}) > \frac{1}{a} , \qquad (11.6)$$

where a is a user-controlled parameter that is proportional to the maximum allowed error on the estimate.

To compute an estimate of the irradiance at x, we compute a weight for all the previously computed irradiance values. For the irradiance values where $w_i > 1/a$ we get:

$$E(x, \vec{n}) \approx \frac{\sum\limits_{i, w_i > 1/a} w_i(x, \vec{n}) E_i(x_i)}{\sum\limits_{i, w_i > 1/a} w_i(x, \vec{n})} . \qquad (11.7)$$

If there is no previously computed irradiance value with a sufficiently high weight, then we compute a new one.

This is the basic principle in the irradiance caching algorithm. There are a number of techniques to make it practical. Firstly, it is very costly to compute the weight for all irradiance values over and over. It is clear that each irradiance value is useful only in a small region of the model. We can precompute the maximum size of this region by ignoring the change in surface normal and only looking at the value of the weight as a function of the distance. The distance at which the weight becomes too low is the maximum distance. It defines a sphere in which the irradiance value is useful. We can place this sphere in an octree structure. This structure is efficient when we want to query if a previously computed irradiance value can be re-used, since we can search down the octree based on our current location and check only those irradiance values that are placed at the voxels of the octree.

Another check for making the irradiance computations practical is to automatically reject all previously computed samples that are above the tangent plane of the current surface location. This is necessary since we may see important objects that are not visible from the samples in front of us.

11.1.1   Irradiance Gradients

It is possible to further improve the quality of the irradiance estimate by including information about the gradient of the irradiance with each irradiance value. The gradient can be estimated from the rays used in Equation 11.1. There is a gradient for both the orientation, $\nabla_r E$, and the position, $\nabla_p E$. Ward and Heckbert [117] derived the formulae for the gradients. They found that the position gradient could be estimated as:

$$\nabla_p E = \sum_{i=1}^{N} \left\{ \vec{T_i} \frac{2\pi}{N} \sum_{j=2}^{M} \frac{\sin\theta_{j_-} \cos^2\theta_{j_-}}{\min(d_{j,i}, d_{j-1,i})} (L_{j,i} - L_{j-1,i}) + \right.$$

$$\left. \vec{T_{i\hat{_-}}} \sum_{j=1}^{M} \frac{\sin\theta_{j_+} - \sin\theta_{j_-}}{\min(d_{j,i}, d_{j,i-1})} (L_{j,i} - L_{j,i-1}) \right\}, \tag{11.8}$$

where

$L_{j,i}$ is the radiance from direction j, i
$d_{j,i}$ is the distance to the object seen in direction j, i
$\vec{T_i}$ is a vector orthogonal to the normal in the direction ϕ_i
$\vec{T_{i\hat{_-}}}$ is a vector orthogonal to the normal in the direction $\phi_{i_-} + \pi/2$
θ_{j_-} is $sin^{-1}\sqrt{j/M}$
θ_{j_+} is $sin^{-1}\sqrt{(j+1)/M}$
ϕ_{i_-} is $2\pi i/N$

The rotational gradient is estimated as:

$$\nabla_r E = \frac{\pi}{MN} \sum_{i=1}^{N} \left\{ \vec{T_i} \sum_{j=1}^{M} -L_{j,i} \tan\theta_j \right\}, \tag{11.9}$$

where $\vec{T_i}$ is a vector orthogonal to the normal in the direction $\phi_i + \pi/2$.

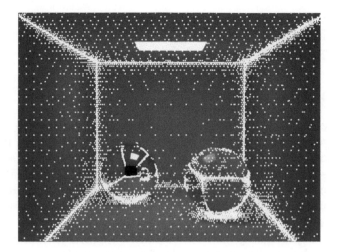

Figure 11.1. The irradiance cache works very well in the box scene. The bright dots superimposed on the darkened box image represent the position at which a new irradiance sample was computed. Notice how large parts of the model can use an interpolated irradiance value.

Using these gradients, the irradiance estimate in Equation 11.7 can be extended as:

$$E(x, \vec{n}) \approx \frac{\sum\limits_{i,w_i>1/a} w_i(x, \vec{n}) \left\{ E_i(x_i) + (x - x_i)\nabla_p E_i + (\vec{n}_i \times \vec{n})\nabla_r E_i \right\}}{\sum\limits_{i,w_i>1/a} w_i(x, \vec{n})}.$$

(11.10)

Figure 11.1 illustrates irradiance caching in the box scene.

11.1.2 Irradiance Caching and Photon Mapping

Photon mapping and irradiance caching work very well together. In the two-pass photon-mapping algorithm, the indirect illumination is soft since the high-frequency caustics contribution is computed using the caustics photon map. This is very important since it eliminates the main cause for error in the irradiance cache. Caustics break the assumptions of the interpolation scheme, and, if they are included in the irradiance cache, the results will be suboptimal.

Furthermore, the photon map can provide additional information to the irradiance sampling. Instead of distributing the sample rays uniformly in

all directions, it is possible to use the approximate representation of the
flux in the photon map to importance-sample in the direction of the bright
indirect sources. This is described in the following section.

11.2   Importance Sampling

Besides providing a radiance estimate, the photon map can be used to
sample the scene more efficiently. Most Monte Carlo approaches use just
the BRDF to select the region to sample. This is fine for specular surfaces,
but for diffuse surfaces it is better to use information about where the light
is coming from. The photon map has this information and the approximate
flux representation has been demonstrated to reduce noise in Monte Carlo
ray tracing [41].

The optimal probability distribution function, $p(x, \vec{\omega}')$, for importance
sampling when integrating the reflected radiance at a surface location, x, is:

$$p(x, \vec{\omega}') \quad \propto \quad f_r(x, \vec{\omega}, \vec{\omega}') L_i(x, \vec{\omega}')(\vec{\omega}' \cdot \vec{n})$$
$$= \quad f_r(x, \vec{\omega}, \vec{\omega}') \frac{d\Phi^2(x, \vec{\omega}')}{dA \, d\vec{\omega}'}. \tag{11.11}$$

We have already seen how the photon map can provide information about
the distribution of the flux $d\Phi$ at x. We can get a sampling of the flux at x
by locating the nearest photons around x. We assume that these photons
all hit x and, as such, are representative of the flux at x.

A simple way to importance-sample according to both the BRDF as
well as the flux distribution from the photons was presented in [41]. The
concept is simple. Consider first importance sampling of a BRDF. Given an
outgoing (reflected) direction we have a function that, given two random
numbers, provides a direction in which to sample the incident radiance.
For a Lambertian surface this function is:

$$\vec{\omega}' = (\theta', \phi') = (cos^{-1}\sqrt{\xi_1}, 2\pi\xi_2) , \tag{11.12}$$

where $\xi_1 \in [0, 1]$ and $\xi_2 \in [0, 1]$ are the two random numbers. This function maps two random numbers in the unit square to a direction on the
hemisphere.

Instead of just uniformly sampling the square with ξ_1 and ξ_2, we can
include further information about the flux. This can be done by dividing
the square into a number of cells. A cell represents a region on the hemisphere (a set of directions). For each cell we accumulate the power of the
photons from the directions represented by the cell. We can find the cell
that a photon maps to by inverting the importance-sampling probability

Figure 11.2. The photon map can be used to importance-sample based on the incident flux as well as the BRDF. The left image shows standard importance sampling using only the BRDF, and the right image shows importance sampling using the photon map. Both images have been rendered using path tracing with 50 paths/pixel.

distribution function used for the BRDF. In case of a diffuse surface this function is:

$$(u, v) = (cos^2\theta, \frac{\phi}{2\pi}) \ . \tag{11.13}$$

Here u, v are the coordinates in the unit square. Based on the recorded power in the cells, we can build a histogram of the power accumulated by the cells. The modified importance sampling proceeds by picking cells in the histogram with a probability proportional to the power accumulated in each cell. A new random position is then selected within the cell and mapped to a direction. A sample ray is then traced in the selected direction to estimate the radiance. The returned estimate should be divided by the probability of picking the cell.

Figure 11.2 gives an example of path tracing using the photon-map-based importance-sampling scheme. Note how the amount of noise in the photon map image is much lower.

It is easy to to use this photon-map importance-sampling method with the irradiance-caching scheme. It is also faster since the histogram only has to be built once for a new irradiance sample.

11.3 Visual Importance

For large models of which only a small part is visible to the observer, it is wasteful to store photons all over the model. In this situation it would be better to inform the photon-tracing step about the position of the observer and the "important" regions of the model.

One technique for doing this is by initially emitting "photons" from the observer to identify the regions of the scene that are important for the final image. This approach was used by Peter and Pietrek [76]. They introduced the term *importons* for photons emitted from the observer. To build the photon map, they used the importance-sampling technique from [41] as presented in the previous section: for each photon traced from a light source they queried the importon map to importance-sample the scattered direction of the photon. Their results demonstrated that they were able to get a higher density photon map in the visually important parts of the model. Unfortunately, their results also suffered from highly varying photon power in the generated photon map due to their unbiased importance-sampling strategy. Intuitively, their method could generate an important photon even by sampling a direction with a low probability. Since importance sampling requires dividing by the probability it is possible to generate high-powered photons that can cause the radiance estimate to be poor.

Another approach to controlling the visual quality of the generated photon map was introduced by Suykens and Willems [105]. They introduced the concept of *density control* for the photon map. The idea in density control is to limit the density of photons in bright regions of the model. These bright regions may not be the visually important parts of the model, and they may even be so bright that the intensity is clipped before being displayed. Both these issues make it valuable to limit the photon density in order to reduce the memory requirements for the photon map. Limiting the photon density locally in bright regions leaves room for more photons in darker regions that are visually important.

Density control works by imposing an upper limit on the number of photons per area (for example, 80,000 photons/m^2). Before storing a photon in the photon map, the current local density is first examined. The new photon is only stored if this density is below the limit. Otherwise, the power of the photon is distributed among the existing *local* photons in the photon map. This ensures that the power received locally will be correct.

Suykens and Willems demonstrated how density control could be used to generate images of similar quality as the standard photon map method, but with the number of photons reduced by a factor of 2–4.

The exciting aspect about density control is that it may be used to answer the question: how many photons are necessary? Suykens and Willems did take the first steps in that direction by investigating the relationship between visual importance and photon density. They computed the local required density based on an importons map similar to Peter and Pietrek [76]. The next step is coupling this work with models from perception to tune the photon map density to the requirements of the observer.

11.3.1   A Three-Pass Technique

A simple three-pass technique [43] that includes visual importance can be made by a simple extension to the two-pass technique presented in Chapter 9.

- The first step is the creation of a visual importance map (or importons map) by emitting visual importance (or importons) from the observer into the model. These importons are traced through at most one diffuse reflection (similar to the rendering step in the two-pass method).

- The second step is building the photon map by tracing photons through the model. This step is enhanced using the visual importance map. Photons are only stored when there is a "sufficient" density of visual importance in the region; otherwise the photon is thrown away. This strategy is clearly biased, but remember that we throw away power only in regions that are classified as unimportant.

- The third step is rendering using the photon map. This step proceeds in the same way as described in Chapter 9.

11.4   Efficient Stratification of Photons

One important technique for improving the quality of the photon map is making sure that the photons are distributed evenly. This improves the radiance estimate and is a good alternative to just using more photons.

It is well known that the accuracy of Monte Carlo integration is improved when clumping of the random samples is avoided. The classic way to reduce clumping is to stratify the samples [81]. This concept is directly applicable to photon mapping. One way to stratify photons is at the light sources. This is easily done by using the projection map, which already is a stratification of the directions at the light source. By alternately selecting projection map cells with "active" objects, there will be at least a minimal stratification of the photons. In [47] it was suggested refining each cell in the projection map further to obtain an even finer level of stratification. Extending this concept to several dimensions is more complicated since the number of photons that are emitted often is unknown.

One way to stratify photons in several dimensions is *quasi-Monte Carlo* (QMC) sampling [70]. QMC sampling uses special quasi-random *low-discrepancy* sequences to distribute the samples. Here quasi-random sampling means that the sequence often can replace the random sequence used in Monte Carlo integration and still give the same result. However, these quasi-random sequences are not random. They are clever constructs used to distribute samples evenly over a domain such that clumping is avoided. The elimination of clumping is measured by the discrepancy of the sequence. Discrepancy is a measure of how well-spaced the samples are. Low discrepancy means that we want to try to maximize the local distance between the samples.

The great advantage about QMC sequences is that they converge as fast as stratified sampling [1] without requiring knowledge about how many samples will be used. Therefore if we use QMC to select the directions in which to emit photons, then we automatically get evenly spaced photons no matter how many photons are emitted. In addition, QMC sequences can provide a stratification of several dimensions. For photon tracing this means that not only are the emitted photons properly stratified, but the first reflected photons will also be stratified. This property has been demonstrated to give better results than randomly emitted photons [54].

The problems with QMC sampling is that it can result in aliasing in the solution, to which the eye is very sensitive. For caustics that are visualized directly, the quasi-random sequences can give very noticeable patterns. A way to avoid this is to add some randomness to the sequence, and this may indeed be a very good way to emit photons.

11.5   Faster Shadows with Shadow Photons

In scenes with many lights or with large area light sources, it can be very costly to compute the direct illumination. This is mainly due to the fact that the visibility of each light is evaluated using shadow rays. Tracing a shadow ray through the scene is costly. Most scenes have large regions that are either fully illuminated or completely in shadow, and it seems wasteful to trace shadow rays for each point to see if there is a shadow. The penumbra regions, for which the light source visibility can be complex, usually cover a much smaller fraction of the scene. Based on these observations it seems natural to try to identify the different regions (shadow, illuminated, or penumbra) of a scene, since this can significantly reduce the number of shadow rays traced.

A simple extension to the photon map makes it possible to classify the different illuminated regions of a model by introducing the concept of *shadow photons* [46]. Shadow photons are created in regions that are in shadow. As shown in Figure 11.3, this is done by tracing photons from the light source through the objects in the model. On all the objects beyond the first one we store shadow photons. We store the shadow photons only on the side of the object that is facing the light source (i.e., the surface normal

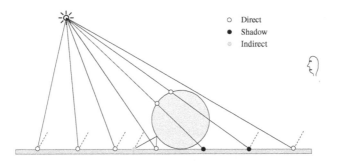

Figure 11.3. Shadow photons are created by tracing photons from the light sources through all objects in the scene and storing them on all the objects beyond the first one. On the first object the stored photon is tagged as representing direct illumination. The remaining photons represent indirect illumination.

points towards the light source). If the normal points away from a light source, then we can trivially conclude that the point is in shadow. With each shadow photon we store the negative power carried by the photon—the reasons for this will become clear later.

In addition to the shadow photons, a few minor modifications to the existing photon map is necessary. Each photon has a bit that is set if the photon comes directly from a light source. Furthermore, all photons are extended to include a light source number (for scenes with less than 2^{14} lights this number can be folded into the flag of the photon structure shown in Chapter 6).

There are several ways in which we can use this extended photon map to speed up the direct illumination computation. These include two fast approximations and one fairly accurate. For all of these methods, we locate the nearest photons in the photon map that come directly from the light source and examine the distribution of shadow photons.

The two fast approximations do not use any shadow rays. One approach is to always compute the full direct illumination from the light source and then add a radiance estimate based on the shadow photons (recall that they carry negative power). This is similar to splatting shadows based on the shadow photon density. Another simple approach is to estimate the visibility of the light source based on the relative amount of direct illumination photons in the located photons:

$$V_{l,fast} = \frac{n_{l,d}}{n_{l,d} + n_{l,s}} . \qquad (11.14)$$

Here $n_{l,d}$ is the number of direct illumination photons, and $n_{l,s}$ is the number of shadow photons received from the light source, l. $V_{l,fast}$ is an

Figure 11.4. 492 shadow photons have been used to identify the penumbra region in this cognac glass model. Even with this low number of photons we are able to get a good estimate of where the shadow boundary is, and this enables a reduction of more than 70% in the number of shadow rays.

estimate of the visibility of l (i.e., the fraction of the light source that is visible from the current location). This fraction is multiplied by the irradiance from a fully visible light source to estimate the actual amount of received irradiance.

Both of the fast approximations can result in blurry shadows if too few photons are used, and for scenes with many light sources it can be costly to obtain good local statistics. For more accurate results it is better to use a conservative approach that traces shadow rays in the *penumbra regions*. The penumbra regions contain the shadow boundaries and they can be identified, since they have a mix of shadow photons and direct illumination photons. This means that if the nearest photons contain both shadow photons and direct illumination photons (even if it is just one of both), then we classify the region as a penumbra region and use shadow rays to evaluate the light source visibility. Tracing shadow rays in the penumbra regions makes sense since the eye is highly sensitive to shadow boundaries.

In Figure 11.4 we show a model of a cognac glass that has been rendered with the identified penumbra region highlighted (the constant colored area around the glass) to illustrate the result of the light source visibility classification. All the other parts of the model have been classified as being either fully illuminated or in shadow. The global photon map uses just 31,994 photons of which only 492 are shadow photons. Even with this approximate representation, the number of shadow rays is reduced more than 70%.

11.6 Precomputed Irradiance

Another extension of the photon map was presented by Christensen [14]. The idea is to precompute the irradiance value for all the photons in the global photon map. In the rendering step, the sampling of the indirect illumination results in many queries to the global photon map, and by having precomputed irradiance values we can make this computation faster, since only the nearest photon is needed.

The precomputed irradiance values increase the size of the photon structure with six bytes (four bytes for a compressed representation of the irradiance and two bytes for the surface normal).

After the photon-tracing step, the irradiance for all photons is computed. This is done using the radiance estimate applied to each photon (by locating the nearest photons around it, etc.). The preprocessing step can be quite costly, and therefore Christensen suggested only precomputing the irradiance for every fourth photon (and use only these photons in the global photon map to compute irradiance).

In the rendering step the queries to the global photon map are simplified since only the nearest photon is needed. To avoid artifacts it is necessary to locate the nearest photon at a surface with a similar normal (this is the reason why the surface normal is stored with the photons).

The precomputed irradiance optimization works for all Lambertian surfaces (for other materials it is still necessary to use the general photon map radiance estimate). Christensen reported very good speedups (a factor of six) for some scenes. Even with a time-consuming precomputation of the irradiance values, the overall speedup was good.

11.7 Parallel Computations

The photon map is very easy to parallelize and very good results can be obtained (see for example [45]).

Since photons are independent they can be traced in parallel using multiple threads and/or multiple machines. Photon tracing is usually pretty fast, so multiple threads on the same machine is often preferable to multiple machines. In the case of multiple machines, it can be simpler to compute the full photon map locally—this may also be faster since the photon map does not have to be transmitted over the network.

Rendering in parallel using the photon map can also be very efficient. As reported in [45] it is even possible to get super-linear speedups using a parallel rendering step. The rendering step is also straightforward to parallelize since rays are independent and can be traced in parallel. The only slightly tricky element of a parallel implementation is the irradiance caching (if it is used), since it requires a locking mechanism to allow dynamic updates as new values are computed.

Basic Monte Carlo Integration

In rendering and in particular global illumination, we often encounter multi-dimensional integration problems of functions (light fields) with many discontinuities. Since these integrals cannot be evaluated efficiently using standard quadrature rules, it is better to use another class of techniques based on Monte Carlo integration.

A.1 The Sample Mean Method

Monte Carlo integration uses random sampling of the function of interest to examine its properties. Given a function, $f(x)$, that we wish to integrate over a one-dimensional domain from a to b:

$$I = \int_a^b f(x)\,dx \ . \tag{A.1}$$

An intuitive way to evaluate this integral is by computing the mean value of $f(x)$ over the interval a to b, and then multiply this mean by the length of the interval $b - a$. For this purpose we can average the values of $f(x)$ at

N locations $\xi_1, \xi_2, \ldots, \xi_N$, where $\xi_{1,\ldots,N}$ are uniformly distributed random numbers between a and b. This gives:

$$I_m = (b-a)\frac{1}{N}\sum_{i=1}^{N} f(\xi_i) \ . \tag{A.2}$$

Here I_m is the Monte Carlo estimate of the integral. As we increase the number of samples, N, this estimate becomes more accurate and in the limit we find that:

$$\lim_{N\to\infty} I_m = I \tag{A.3}$$

How fast does the estimator I_m converge towards the correct result I? To answer this question we can compute the variance σ^2 of our estimate I_m:

$$\sigma^2 = \frac{1}{N}\left(\int_a^b f^2(x)\,dx - I^2\right) \ . \tag{A.4}$$

Since the standard deviation σ is the square root of the variance, we find that:

$$\sigma \propto \frac{1}{\sqrt{N}} \ . \tag{A.5}$$

In other words to halve the error we must quadruple the number of samples! This is the caveat of Monte Carlo integration. It is very easy to use on most problems, but the convergence is slow. However, for high-dimensional integrals (such as those in rendering), the convergence is often better than any other method can give [81].

We can also estimate the variance σ_s^2 of our sampling distribution:

$$\sigma_s^2 = \frac{1}{N-1}\sum_{i=1}^{N}(f(\xi_i) - I_m)^2 \ . \tag{A.6}$$

This estimate contains the factor $1/(N-1)$, which shows that the variance (the noise) of our samples converges as slowly as the variance of our estimate.

Fortunately there are several variance-reduction techniques available.

A.2   Variance-Reduction Techniques

To improve the quality of our estimate we must reduce the variance. The basic strategy is to use as much knowledge as we have about the function that we wish to integrate.

A technique that is very commonly used in rendering is *importance sampling*. The idea in importance sampling is to concentrate the samples of the function in the important parts of the function. For example, if the function has a high value in a small interval, then it pays to use more samples in this interval.

For this purpose we construct a probability density function, p.d.f., that "has the same shape" as $f(x)$. Given a stochastic variable X with p.d.f. $p(x)$, $x \in [a, b]$ such that $p(x) > 0$ when $f(x) \neq 0$ we find that:

$$I = \int_a^b \frac{f(x)}{p(x)} p(x) \, dx = E\left\{ \frac{f(X)}{p(X)} \right\} \qquad (A.7)$$

At first glance this may not seem very useful. The power of this method relies on the ability to construct random samples $\psi_1, \dots, \psi_N$ from X. This gives the following estimator I_{mi} for I:

$$I_{mi} = \frac{1}{N} \sum_{i=1}^{N} \frac{f(\psi_i)}{p(\psi_i)} \qquad (A.8)$$

The variance of this estimate will still be proportional to $1/N$, but by picking a good p.d.f. we can make it arbitrarily low. The optimal p.d.f., $p_{opt}(x)$, is:

$$p_{opt}(x) = \frac{f(x)}{I} . \qquad (A.9)$$

With this p.d.f. the variance is always zero! Unfortunately, it requires knowledge of I, which is the quantity that we are trying to compute. In general we can improve our estimate by adding small knowledge to the sampling distribution. In rendering it may be that we know that a certain object is brighter than the rest, and we can improve our sampling by sending more rays towards this object.

Another powerful variance-reduction technique is *stratified sampling*. The simplest form of stratified sampling divides the domain $[a, b]$ into N subdomains. In each subdomain we place one sample. It can be shown [81] that this simple technique cannot result in higher variance than the random sampling approach, and if the function is smooth it often results in significantly better estimates. The variance is proportional to $1/N^2$, which is much better than naive random sampling. As such, stratified sampling should be used whenever possible! It is only when the number of samples to be taken is unknown that stratified sampling is problematic.

There are several other variance-reduction techniques available for Monte Carlo integration. See the classic book by Rubinstein [81] for a good overview.

A Photon Map
Implementation in C++

This appendix contains a full C++ implementation of a photon map class. This class can be integrated into any ray tracer to provide the basic tool to add caustics and simple global illumination. The only additional code to add to such a ray tracer is photon tracing (emission of photons from the lights, and scattering and storing of photons by the materials). These photons can then be handled by the photon map implementation provided below. The usage of the implementation should be fairly easy to understand.

```
1  //-------------------------------------------------------------------------
   // photonmap.cc
   // An example implementation of the photon map data structure
   //
   // Henrik Wann Jensen - February 2001
   //-------------------------------------------------------------------------

   #include <stdio.h>
   #include <stdlib.h>
10 #include <string.h>
   #include <math.h>
```

```
     /* This is the photon
      * The power is not compressed so the
      * size is 28 bytes
      */
     //**********************
     typedef struct Photon {
20   //**********************
       float pos[3];                  // photon position
       short plane;                   // splitting plane for kd-tree
       unsigned char theta, phi;      // incoming direction
       float power[3];                // photon power (uncompressed)
     } Photon;


     /* This structure is used only to locate the
      * nearest photons
30   */
     //****************************
     typedef struct NearestPhotons {
     //****************************
       int max;
       int found;
       int got_heap;
       float pos[3];
       float *dist2;
       const Photon **index;
40   } NearestPhotons;


     /* This is the Photon_map class
      */
     //****************
     class Photon_map {
     //****************
     public:
       Photon_map( int max_phot );
50     ~Photon_map();

       void store(
         const float power[3],        // photon power
         const float pos[3],          // photon position
         const float dir[3] );        // photon direction

       void scale_photon_power(
         const float scale );         // 1/(number of emitted photons)

60     void balance(void);            // balance the kd-tree (before use!)

       void irradiance_estimate(
         float irrad[3],              // returned irradiance
         const float pos[3],          // surface position
         const float normal[3],       // surface normal at pos
         const float max_dist,        // max distance to look for photons
         const int nphotons ) const;  // number of photons to use

       void locate_photons(
70       NearestPhotons *const np,     // np is used to locate the photons
         const int index ) const;     // call with index = 1

       void photon_dir(
         float *dir,                  // direction of photon (returned)
         const Photon *p ) const;     // the photon

     private:

       void balance_segment(
80       Photon **pbal,
         Photon **porg,
         const int index,
```

```
       const int start,
       const int end );

     void median_split(
       Photon **p,
       const int start,
       const int end,
90     const int median,
       const int axis );

     Photon *photons;

     int stored_photons;
     int half_stored_photons;
     int max_photons;
     int prev_scale;

100    float costheta[256];
     float sintheta[256];
     float cosphi[256];
     float sinphi[256];

     float bbox_min[3];      // use bbox_min;
     float bbox_max[3];      // use bbox_max;
   };


110
   /* This is the constructor for the photon map.
    * To create the photon map it is necessary to specify the
    * maximum number of photons that will be stored
    */
   //*********************************************
   Photon_map :: Photon_map( const int max_phot )
   //*********************************************
   {
     stored_photons = 0;
120   prev_scale = 1;
     max_photons = max_phot;

     photons = (Photon*)malloc( sizeof( Photon ) * ( max_photons+1 ) );

     if (photons == NULL) {
       fprintf(stderr,"Out of memory initializing photon map\n");
       exit(-1);
     }

130   bbox_min[0] = bbox_min[1] = bbox_min[2] = 1e8f;
     bbox_max[0] = bbox_max[1] = bbox_max[2] = -1e8f;

     //----------------------------------------
     // initialize direction conversion tables
     //----------------------------------------

     for (int i=0; i<256; i++) {
       double angle = double(i)*(1.0/256.0)*M_PI;
       costheta[i] = cos( angle );
140     sintheta[i] = sin( angle );
       cosphi[i]   = cos( 2.0*angle );
       sinphi[i]   = sin( 2.0*angle );
     }
   }


   //************************
   Photon_map :: ~Photon_map()
   //************************
150 {
     free( photons );
   }
```

```
      /* photon_dir returns the direction of a photon
       */
      //*****************************************************************
      void Photon_map :: photon_dir( float *dir, const Photon *p ) const
      //*****************************************************************
160   {
        dir[0] = sintheta[p->theta]*cosphi[p->phi];
        dir[1] = sintheta[p->theta]*sinphi[p->phi];
        dir[2] = costheta[p->theta];
      }


      /* irradiance_estimate computes an irradiance estimate
       * at a given surface position
       */
170   //********************************************
      void Photon_map :: irradiance_estimate(
        float irrad[3],                 // returned irradiance
        const float pos[3],             // surface position
        const float normal[3],          // surface normal at pos
        const float max_dist,           // max distance to look for photons
        const int nphotons ) const      // number of photons to use
      //********************************************
      {
        irrad[0] = irrad[1] = irrad[2] = 0.0;
180
        NearestPhotons np;
        np.dist2 = (float*)alloca( sizeof(float)*(nphotons+1) );
        np.index = (const Photon**)alloca( sizeof(Photon*)*(nphotons+1) );

        np.pos[0] = pos[0]; np.pos[1] = pos[1]; np.pos[2] = pos[2];
        np.max = nphotons;
        np.found = 0;
        np.got_heap = 0;
        np.dist2[0] = max_dist*max_dist;
190
        // locate the nearest photons
        locate_photons( &np, 1 );

        // if less than 8 photons return
        if (np.found<8)
          return;

        float pdir[3];

200   // sum irradiance from all photons
        for (int i=1; i<=np.found; i++) {
          const Photon *p = np.index[i];
          // the photon_dir call and following if can be omitted (for speed)
          // if the scene does not have any thin surfaces
          photon_dir( pdir, p );
          if ( (pdir[0]*normal[0]+pdir[1]*normal[1]+pdir[2]*normal[2]) < 0.0f ) {
            irrad[0] += p->power[0];
            irrad[1] += p->power[1];
            irrad[2] += p->power[2];
          }
210   }

        const float tmp=(1.0f/M_PI)/(np.dist2[0]);   // estimate of density

        irrad[0] *= tmp;
        irrad[1] *= tmp;
        irrad[2] *= tmp;
      }

220
      /* locate_photons finds the nearest photons in the
       * photon map given the parameters in np
       */
      //****************************************
```

```
     void Photon_map :: locate_photons(
       NearestPhotons *const np,
       const int index ) const
     //******************************************
     {
230    const Photon *p = &photons[index];
       float dist1;

       if (index<half_stored_photons) {
         dist1 = np->pos[ p->plane ] - p->pos[ p->plane ];

         if (dist1>0.0) { // if dist1 is positive search right plane
           locate_photons( np, 2*index+1 );
           if ( dist1*dist1 < np->dist2[0] )
             locate_photons( np, 2*index );
240      } else {          // dist1 is negative search left first
           locate_photons( np, 2*index );
           if ( dist1*dist1 < np->dist2[0] )
             locate_photons( np, 2*index+1 );
         }
       }

       // compute squared distance between current photon and np->pos

       dist1 = p->pos[0] - np->pos[0];
250    float dist2 = dist1*dist1;
       dist1 = p->pos[1] - np->pos[1];
       dist2 += dist1*dist1;
       dist1 = p->pos[2] - np->pos[2];
       dist2 += dist1*dist1;

       if ( dist2 < np->dist2[0] ) {
         // we found a photon :) Insert it in the candidate list

         if ( np->found < np->max ) {
260        // heap is not full; use array
           np->found++;
           np->dist2[np->found] = dist2;
           np->index[np->found] = p;
         } else {
           int j,parent;

           if (np->got_heap==0) { // Do we need to build the heap?
             // Build heap
             float dst2;
270          const Photon *phot;
             int half_found = np->found>>1;
             for ( int k=half_found; k>=1; k-- ) {
               parent=k;
               phot = np->index[k];
               dst2 = np->dist2[k];
               while ( parent <= half_found ) {
                 j = parent+parent;
                 if (j<np->found && np->dist2[j]<np->dist2[j+1])
                   j++;
280              if (dst2>=np->dist2[j])
                   break;
                 np->dist2[parent] = np->dist2[j];
                 np->index[parent] = np->index[j];
                 parent=j;
               }
               np->dist2[parent] = dst2;
               np->index[parent] = phot;
             }
             np->got_heap = 1;
290        }

           // insert new photon into max heap
           // delete largest element, insert new, and reorder the heap

           parent=1;
```

```
         j = 2;
         while ( j <= np->found ) {
           if ( j < np->found && np->dist2[j] < np->dist2[j+1] )
             j++;
300        if ( dist2 > np->dist2[j] )
             break;
           np->dist2[parent] = np->dist2[j];
           np->index[parent] = np->index[j];
           parent = j;
           j += j;
         }
           if ( dist2 < np->dist2[parent] {
             np->index[parent] = p;
             np->dist2[parent] = dist2;
310        }
       np->dist2[0] = np->dist2[1];
     }
   }
 }


   /* store puts a photon into the flat array that will form
    * the final kd-tree.
    *
320 * Call this function to store a photon.
    */
   //**************************
   void Photon_map :: store(
     const float power[3],
     const float pos[3],
     const float dir[3] )
   //**************************
   {
     if (stored_photons>=max_photons)
330    return;

     stored_photons++;
     Photon *const node = &photons[stored_photons];

     for (int i=0; i<3; i++) {
       node->pos[i] = pos[i];

       if (node->pos[i] < bbox_min[i])
         bbox_min[i] = node->pos[i];
340    if (node->pos[i] > bbox_max[i])
         bbox_max[i] = node->pos[i];

       node->power[i] = power[i];
     }

     int theta = int( acos(dir[2])*(256.0/M_PI) );
     if (theta>255)
       node->theta = 255;
     else
350    node->theta = (unsigned char)theta;

     int phi = int( atan2(dir[1],dir[0])*(256.0/(2.0*M_PI)) );
     if (phi>255)
       node->phi = 255;
     else if (phi<0)
       node->phi = (unsigned char)(phi+256);
     else
       node->phi = (unsigned char)phi;
   }
360

   /* scale_photon_power is used to scale the power of all
    * photons once they have been emitted from the light
    * source. scale = 1/(#emitted photons).
    * Call this function after each light source is processed.
    */
```

```
//**********************************************************
void Photon_map :: scale_photon_power( const float scale )
//**********************************************************
{
    for (int i=prev_scale; i<=stored_photons; i++) {
        photons[i].power[0] *= scale;
        photons[i].power[1] *= scale;
        photons[i].power[2] *= scale;
    }
    prev_scale = stored_photons+1;
}


/* balance creates a left-balanced kd-tree from the flat photon array.
 * This function should be called before the photon map
 * is used for rendering.
 */
//*****************************
void Photon_map :: balance(void)
//*****************************
{
    if (stored_photons>1) {
        // allocate two temporary arrays for the balancing procedure
        Photon **pa1 = (Photon**)malloc(sizeof(Photon*)*(stored_photons+1));
        Photon **pa2 = (Photon**)malloc(sizeof(Photon*)*(stored_photons+1));

        for (int i=0; i<=stored_photons; i++)
            pa2[i] = &photons[i];

        balance_segment( pa1, pa2, 1, 1, stored_photons );
        free(pa2);

        // reorganize balanced kd-tree (make a heap)
        int d, j=1, foo=1;
        Photon foo_photon = photons[j];

        for (int i=1; i<=stored_photons; i++) {
            d=pa1[j]-photons;
            pa1[j] = NULL;
            if (d != foo)
                photons[j] = photons[d];
            else {
                photons[j] = foo_photon;

                if (i<stored_photons) {
                    for (;foo<=stored_photons; foo++)
                        if (pa1[foo] != NULL)
                            break;
                    foo_photon = photons[foo];
                    j = foo;
                }
                continue;
            }
            j = d;
        }
        free(pa1);
    }

    half_stored_photons = stored_photons/2-1;
}


#define swap(ph,a,b) { Photon *ph2=ph[a]; ph[a]=ph[b]; ph[b]=ph2; }

// median_split splits the photon array into two separate
// pieces around the median, with all photons below
// the median in the lower half and all photons above
// the median in the upper half. The comparison
// criteria is the axis (indicated by the axis parameter)
// (inspired by routine in "Algorithms in C++" by Sedgewick)
//**************************************************************
```

```
     void Photon_map :: median_split(
       Photon **p,
440    const int start,            // start of photon block in array
       const int end,              // end of photon block in array
       const int median,           // desired median number
       const int axis )            // axis to split along
     //****************************************************************
     {
       int left = start;
       int right = end;

       while ( right > left ) {
450      const float v = p[right]->pos[axis];
         int i=left-1;
         int j=right;
         for (;;) {
           while ( p[++i]->pos[axis] < v )
             ;
           while ( p[--j]->pos[axis] > v && j>left )
             ;
           if ( i >= j )
             break;
460        swap(p,i,j);
         }

         swap(p,i,right);
         if ( i >= median )
           right=i-1;
         if ( i <= median )
           left=i+1;
       }
     }
470

     // See "Realistic Image Synthesis using Photon Mapping" Chapter 6
     // for an explanation of this function
     //****************************
     void Photon_map :: balance_segment(
       Photon **pbal,
       Photon **porg,
       const int index,
       const int start,
480    const int end )
     //****************************
     {
       //--------------------
       // compute new median
       //--------------------

       int median=1;
       while ((4*median) <= (end-start+1))
         median += median;
490
       if ((3*median) <= (end-start+1)) {
         median += median;
         median += start-1;
       } else
         median = end-median+1;

       //-------------------------
       // find axis to split along
       //-------------------------
500
       int axis=2;
       if ((bbox_max[0]-bbox_min[0])>(bbox_max[1]-bbox_min[1]) &&
           (bbox_max[0]-bbox_min[0])>(bbox_max[2]-bbox_min[2]))
         axis=0;
       else if ((bbox_max[1]-bbox_min[1])>(bbox_max[2]-bbox_min[2]))
         axis=1;

       //------------------------------------------
```

```
      // partition photon block around the median
510   //-------------------------------------------

      median_split( porg, start, end, median, axis );

      pbal[ index ] = porg[ median ];
      pbal[ index ]->plane = axis;

      //-----------------------------------------------
      // recursively balance the left and right block
      //-----------------------------------------------
520
      if ( median > start ) {
        // balance left segment
        if ( start < median-1 ) {
          const float tmp=bbox_max[axis];
          bbox_max[axis] = pbal[index]->pos[axis];
          balance_segment( pbal, porg, 2*index, start, median-1 );
          bbox_max[axis] = tmp;
        } else {
          pbal[ 2*index ] = porg[start];
530     }
      }

      if ( median < end ) {
        // balance right segment
        if ( median+1 < end ) {
          const float tmp = bbox_min[axis];
          bbox_min[axis] = pbal[index]->pos[axis];
          balance_segment( pbal, porg, 2*index+1, median+1, end );
          bbox_min[axis] = tmp;
540     } else {
          pbal[ 2*index+1 ] = porg[end];
        }
      }
    }
```

C

A Cognac Glass Model

This appendix contains the data used for the cognac glass model which has appeared in several images in this book. It is a good model for simulating caustics.

The data is given as three contour curves. There is a contour for the cognac-air interface, the glass-air interface, and the cognac-glass interface. The three interfaces are necessary to properly account for Fresnel effects. Modeling a volume of cognac inside a glass with a tiny bit of air between the two would not be correct.

The contour curves can be typed into most modeling programs. The cognac glass is then created by rotating this curve around the center axis (radius=0).

The data for the cognac-air interface contour is:

Height	Radius
6.5	3.8
6.48	3.76
6.45	3.75
6.45	0

The data for the glass-cognac interface contour is:

Height	Radius	Height	Radius
6.50	3.80	cont'd	cont'd
6.05	3.79	4.33	2.70
5.60	3.73	3.95	1.98
5.15	3.55	3.58	1.06
4.70	3.20	3.20	0.00

The data for the glass-air interface contour is:

Height	Radius	Height	Radius	Height	Radius
0.90000	0.000000	cont'd	cont'd	cont'd	cont'd
0.77500	0.087946	1.00000	0.500000	10.16250	2.807188
0.65000	0.167857	1.30000	0.500000	10.55000	2.700000
0.52500	0.338839	1.60000	0.500000	10.57250	2.695273
0.40000	0.700000	1.90000	0.500000	10.59500	2.692188
0.31250	1.178594	2.20000	0.500000	10.61750	2.690508
0.22500	1.821250	2.27500	0.515031	10.64000	2.690000
0.13750	2.465781	2.35000	0.556750	10.65375	2.690469
0.05000	2.950000	2.42500	0.620094	10.66750	2.688750
0.03775	2.981703	2.50000	0.700000	10.68125	2.680156
0.02550	2.993875	2.81250	1.149888	10.69500	2.660000
0.01325	3.009109	3.12500	1.710119	10.69625	2.650594
0.00100	3.050000	3.43750	2.277790	10.69750	2.633250
0.00075	3.062539	3.75000	2.750000	10.69875	2.616781
0.00050	3.088437	4.01250	3.048824	10.70000	2.610000
0.00025	3.113867	4.27500	3.294114	10.66250	2.592930
0.00000	3.125000	4.53750	3.492347	10.62500	2.595313
0.05000	3.218750	4.80000	3.650000	10.58750	2.607539
0.10000	3.250000	5.22500	3.831752	10.55000	2.620000
0.15000	3.218750	5.65000	3.937946	10.16250	2.724063
0.20000	3.125000	6.07500	3.987667	9.77500	2.840625
0.36250	2.497187	6.50000	4.000000	9.38750	2.966875
0.52500	1.642500	7.12500	3.916016	9.00000	3.100000
0.68750	0.885313	7.75000	3.709375	8.37500	3.332422
0.85000	0.550000	8.37500	3.448047	7.75000	3.559375
0.88750	0.540078	9.00000	3.200000	7.12500	3.731641
0.92500	0.523125	9.38750	3.063750	6.50000	3.800000
0.96250	0.507109	9.77500	2.930625		

Bibliography

[1] Masaki Aono and Ryutarou Ohbuchi. "Quasi-Monte Carlo rendering with adaptive sampling." Technical Report RT0167, IBM Tokyo Research Laboratory, 1996.

[2] James Arvo. Backward Ray Tracing. In *Developments in Ray Tracing, SIGGRAPH '86 Seminar Notes*, volume 12, August 1986.

[3] James Arvo and David B. Kirk. "Particle Transport and Image Synthesis." *Computer Graphics (Proc. SIGGRAPH '90)* 24(4): 63–66 (August 1990).

[4] Franz Aurenhammer. "Voronoi diagrams—a survey of a fundamental geometric data structure." *ACM Computing Surveys* 23(3): (September 1991).

[5] Jon L. Bentley. "Multidimensional binary search trees used for associative searching." *Communications of the ACM* 18(9): 509–517 (1975).

[6] Jon L. Bentley. "Multidimensional binary search trees in database applications." *IEEE Trans. on Soft. Eng.* 5(4): 333–340 (July 1979).

[7] Jon L. Bentley and Jerome H. Friedman. "Data structures for range searching." *Computing Surveys* 11(4): 397–409 (1979).

[8] Jon L. Bentley, Bruce W. Weide, and Andrew C. Yao. "Optimal expected-time algorithm for closest point problems." *ACM Trans. on Math. Soft.* 6(4): 563–580 (1980).

[9] Philippe Blasi, Bertrand Le Saec, and Christophe Schlick. "A rendering algorithm for discrete volume density objects." *Computer Gaphics Forum (Eurographics '93)* 12(3): 201–210 (1993).

[10] James F. Blinn. "Models of light reflection for computer synthesized pictures." *Computer Graphics (Proc. SIGGRAPH '77)* 11(2): 192–198 (July 1977).

[11] Craig Bohren and Donald Huffman. *Absorption and Scattering of Light by Small Particles.* New York: John Wiley & Sons, 1983.

[12] Jed Z. Buchwald. *The Rise of the Wave Theory of Light.* Chicago: The University of Chicago Press, 1989.

[13] Shenchang Eric Chen, Holly E. Rushmeier, Gavin Miller, and Douglass Turner. "A progressive multi-pass method for global illumination." *Computer Graphics (Proc. SIGGRAPH '91)* 25(4): 165–174 (July 1991).

[14] Per H. Christensen. "Faster photon map global illumination." *Journal of Graphics Tools* 4(3): 1–10 (1999).

[15] Per H. Christensen, Eric J. Stollnitz, David H. Salesin, and Tony D. DeRose. "Global illumination of glossy environments using wavelets and importance." *ACM Transactions on Graphics* 15(1): 37–71 (January 1996).

[16] Michael F. Cohen and Donald P. Greenberg. "The Hemi-Cube: A radiosity solution for complex environments." *Computer Graphics (Proc. SIGGRAPH '85)* 19(3): 31–40 (August 1985).

[17] Michael F. Cohen and John R. Wallace. *Radiosity and Realistic Image Synthesis.* San Diego, CA: Academic Press, 1993.

[18] Steven Collins. "Adaptive splatting for specular to diffuse light transport." In *Fifth Eurographics Workshop on Rendering*, pp. 119–135, June 1994.

[19] Steven Collins. *Wavefront Tracking for Global Illumination Solutions.* PhD thesis, Dept. Computer Science, Trinity College Dublin, 1996.

[20] Robert L. Cook. "Stochastic sampling in computer graphics." *ACM Transactions on Graphics* 5(1): 51–72 (Jan 1986).

[21] Robert L. Cook, Thomas Porter, and Loren Carpenter. "Distributed ray tracing." *Computer Graphics (Proc. SIGGRAPH '84)* 18(3): 137–145 (July 1984).

[22] Thomas H. Cormen, Charles E. Leiserson, and Ronald L. Rivest. *Introduction to Algorithms.* Cambridge, MA: MIT Press, 1989.

[23] Julie Dorsey, Alan Edelman, Henrik Wann Jensen, Justin Legakis, and Hans Køhling Pedersen. "Modeling and rendering of weathered stone." In *Proceedings of SIGGRAPH 99, Computer Graphics Proceedings, Annual Conference Series*, edited by Alyn Rockwood, pp. 225–234, Reading, MA: Addison-Wesley, 1999.

[24] Philip Dutré. *Mathematical Frameworks and Monte Carlo Algorithms for Global Illumination in Computer Graphics.* PhD thesis, University of Leuven, 1998.

[25] Ronald Fedkiw, Jos Stam, and Henrik Wann Jensen. "Visual simulation of smoke." In *Proceedings of SIGGRAPH 2001, Computer Graphics Proceedings, Annual Conference Series*, to appear.

[26] Andrew S. Glassner. "Space subdivision for fast ray tracing." *IEEE Computer Graphics and Applications* 4(10): 15–22 (October 1984).

[27] Andrew S. Glassner. *An Introduction to Ray Tracing.* London: Academic Press, 1989.

[28] Andrew S. Glassner. *Principles of Digital Image Sythesis.* Los Altos: Morgan Kaufmann, 1995.

[29] Cindy M. Goral, Kenneth E. Torrance, Donald P. Greenberg, and Bennett Battaile. "Modelling the interaction of light between diffuse surfaces." *Computer Graphics (Proc. SIGGRAPH '84)* 18(3): 212–22 (July 1984).

[30] Steven J. Gortler, Peter Schroder, Michael F. Cohen, and Pat Hanrahan. "Wavelet radiosity." In *Proceedings of SIGGRAPH '93, Computer Graphics Proceedings, Annual Conference Series*, edited by James T. Kajiya, pp. 221–230, New York: ACM Press, 1993.

[31] Roy Hall. *Illumination and Color in Computer Generated Imagery.* New York: Springer-Verlag, 1989.

[32] Pat Hanrahan and Wolfgang Krueger. "Reflection from layered surfaces due to subsurface scattering." In *Proceedings of SIGGRAPH '93, Computer Graphics Proceedings, Annual Conference Series*, edited by James T. Kajiya, pp. 165–174, New York: ACM Press, 1993.

[33] Pat Hanrahan, David Salzman, and Larry Aupperle. "A rapid hierarchical radiosity algorithm." *Computer Graphics (Proc. SIGGRAPH '91)* 25(4): 197–206 (July 1991).

[34] Paul S. Heckbert. "Adaptive radiosity textures for bidirectional ray tracing." *Computer Graphics (Proc. SIGGRAPH '90)* 24(4): 145–154 (August 1990).

[35] L. G. Henyey and J. L. Greenstein. "Diffuse radiation in the galaxy." *Astrophysics Journal*, 93: 70–83, 1941.

[36] Ellis Horowitz, Sartaj Sahni, and Susan Anderson-Freed. *Fundamentals of Data Structures in C.* New York: W. H. Freeman & Co., 1993.

[37] David S. Immel, Michael F. Cohen, and Donald P. Greenberg. "A radiosity method for non-diffuse environments." *Computer Graphics (Proc. SIGGRAPH '86)* 20(4): 133–142 (August 1986).

[38] American National Standard Institute. *Nomenclature and Definitions for Illumination Engineering.* ANSI report, ANSI/IES RP-16-1986, 1986.

[39] Frederik W. Jansen. "Data structures for ray tracing." In *Data Structures for Raster Graphics*, edited by L. R. A. Kessener, F.J. Peters, and M. L. P. van Lierop, pp. 57–73, Berlin: Springer-Verlag, 1985.

[40] Henrik Wann Jensen. *Global illumination via bidirektional Monte Carlo ray tracing.* Master's thesis, Technical University of Denmark, 1993.

[41] Henrik Wann Jensen. "Importance driven path tracing using the photon map." In *Eurographics Rendering Workshop 1995*, edited by P. Hanrahan and W. Purgathofer, pp. 326–335, Eurographics, June 1995.

[42] Henrik Wann Jensen. "Global illumination using photon maps." In *Eurographics Rendering Workshop 1996*, edited by Xavier Pueyo and Peter Schröder, pp. 21–30, Vienna: Springer-Verlag, 1996.

[43] Henrik Wann Jensen. *The photon map in global illumination.* PhD thesis, Technical University of Denmark, September 1996.

[44] Henrik Wann Jensen. "Rendering caustics on non-Lambertian surfaces." In *Graphics Interface '96*, edited by Wayne A. Davis and Richard Bartels, pp. 116–121, Canadian Information Processing Society, Canadian Human-Computer Communications Society, May 1996.

[45] Henrik Wann Jensen. *Parallel global illumination using photon mapping.* SIGGRAPH 2000 Course Notes, New York: ACM Press, July 2000.

[46] Henrik Wann Jensen and Niels J. Christensen. "Efficiently rendering shadows using the photon map." In *Compugraphics '95*, edited by Harold P. Santo, pp. 285–291, December 1995.

[47] Henrik Wann Jensen and Niels Jørgen Christensen. "Photon maps in bidirectional Monte Carlo ray tracing of complex objects." *Computers & Graphics* 19(2): 215–224 (March 1995).

[48] Henrik Wann Jensen and Per H. Christensen. "Efficient simulation of light transport in scenes with participating media using photon maps." In *Proceedings of SIGGRAPH '98, Computer Graphics Proceedings, Annual Conference Series*, edited by Michael Cohen, pp. 311–320, Reading, MA: Addison Wesley, 1998.

[49] Henrik Wann Jensen and Stephen Duck. "The light of Mies van der Rohe, July 2000." Animation in SIGGRAPH'2000 Electronic Theater.

[50] Henrik Wann Jensen, Justin Legakis, and Julie Dorsey. "Rendering of wet materials." In *Rendering Techniques '99*, edited by D. Lischinski and G. W. Larson, Vienna: Springer-Verlag, 1999.

[51] Henrik Wann Jensen, Steve Marschner, Marc Levoy, and Pat Hanrahan. "A practical model for subsurface light transport." In *Proceedings of SIGGRAPH 2001, Computer Graphics Proceedings, Annual Conference Series*, to appear.

[52] James T. Kajiya. "The rendering equation." *Computer Graphics (Proc. SIGGRAPH '86)* 20(4): 143–150 (August 1986).

[53] Timothy L. Kay and James T. Kajiya. "Ray tracing complex scenes." *Computer Graphics (Proc. SIGGRAPH '86)* 20(4): 269–278 (August 1986).

[54] Alexander Keller. "Quasi-Monte Carlo radiosity." In *Eurographics Rendering Workshop 1996*, edited by Xavier Pueyo and Peter Schröder, pp. 101–110, Vienna: Spinger-Verlag, 1996.

[55] Krzysztof S. Klimanszewski and Thomas W. Sederberg. "Faster ray tracing using adaptive grids." *IEEE Computer Graphics & Applications* 17(1): 42–51 (January-February 1997).

[56] Eric P. Lafortune. *Mathematical Models and Monte Carlo Algorithms for Physcially Based Rendering.* PhD thesis, University of Leuven, 1996.

[57] Eric P. Lafortune and Yves D. Willems. "Bidirectional path tracing." In *Compugraphics '93*, pp. 95–104, 1993.

[58] Eric P. Lafortune and Yves D. Willems. "A 5D tree to reduce the variance of Monte Carlo ray tracing." In *Eurographics Rendering Workshop 1995*, edited by Patrick Hanrahan and Werner Purgathofer, pp. 11–20, Eurographics, June 1995.

[59] Eric P. F. Lafortune, Sing-Choong Foo, Kenneth E. Torrance, and Donald P. Greenberg. "Non-linear approximation of reflectance functions." In *Proceedings of SIGGRAPH '97, Computer Graphics Proceedings, Annual Conference Series*, edited by Turner Whitted, pp. 117–126, Reading, MA: Addison Wesley, 1997. ISBN 0-89791-896-7.

[60] Mark E. Lee, Richard A. Redner, and Samuel P. Uselton. "Statistically optimized sampling for distributed ray tracing." *Computer Graphics (Proc. SIGGRAPH '85)* 19(3): 61–67 (July 1985).

[61] Marc Levoy, Kari Pulli, Brian Curless, Szymon Rusinkiewicz, David Koller, Lucas Pereira, Matt Ginzton, Sean Anderson, James Davis, Jeremy Ginsberg, Jonathan Shade, and Duane Fulk. "The digital michelangelo project: 3d scanning of large statues." In *Proceedings of SIGGRAPH 2000, Computer Graphics Proceedings, Annual Conference Series*, edited by Kurt Akeley, pp. 131–144, Reading, MA: Addison Wesley, 2000.

[62] Robert Lewis. "Making shaders more physically plausible." In *Fourth Eurographics Workshop on Rendering*, edited by Michael F. Cohen, Claude Puech, and Francois Sillion, pp. 47–62, Eurographics, June 1993.

[63] Daniel Lischinski, Filippo Tampieri, and Donald P. Greenberg. "Discontinuity meshing for accurate radiosity." *IEEE Computer Graphics and Applications* 12(6): 25–39 (November 1992).

[64] Nicholas Metropolis, Arianna Rosenbluth, Marshall Rosenbluth, Augusta Teller, and Edward Teller. "Equation of state calculations by fast computing machines." *The Journal of Chemical Physics* 21(6): 1087–1092 (1953).

[65] Gustav Mie. "Beiträge zur Optik trüber Medien, speziell kolloidaler Metalllösungen." *Annalen der Physik* 25: 377–445 (1908).

[66] M. Minnaert. *Light and Color in the Outdoors.* Berlin: Springer-Verlag, 1993.

[67] Don P. Mitchell. "Generating antialiased images at low sampling densities." *Computer Graphics (Proc. SIGGRAPH '87)* 21(4): 65–72 (July 1987).

[68] Karol Myszkowski. "Lighting reconstruction using fast and adaptive density estimation techniques." In *Eurographics Rendering Workshop 1997*, edited by Julie Dorsey and Philipp Slusallek, pp. 251–262, Vienna: Springer-Verlag, 1997.

[69] F. E. Nicodemus, J. C. Richmond, J. J. Hsia, I. W. Ginsberg, and T. Limperis. *Geometric considerations and nomenclature for reflectance.* Monograph 161, National Bureau of Standards (US), October 1977.

[70] Harald Niederreiter. *Random Number Generation and Quasi-Monte Carlo Methods.* Philadelphia: SIAM, 1992.

[71] T. Nishita, I. Okamura, and E. Nakamae. "Shading models for point and linear sources." *ACM Transactions on Graphics* 4(2): 124–146 (April 1985).

[72] Michael Oren and Shree K. Nayar. "Generalization of Lambert's reflectance model." In *Proceedings of SIGGRAPH '94, Computer Graphics Proceedings, Annual Conference Series* edited by Andrew Glassner, pp. 239–246, New York: ACM Press, July 1994.

[73] James Painter and Kenneth Sloan. "Antialiased ray tracing by adaptive progressive refinement." *Computer Graphics (Proc. SIGGRAPH '89)* 23(3): 281–288 (July 1989).

[74] Sumanta N. Pattanaik. *Computational Methods for Global Illumination and Visualisation of Complex 3D Environments.* PhD thesis, Birla Institute of Technology & Science, 1993.

[75] Mark J. Pavicic. "Convenient anti-aliasing filters that minimize bumpy sampling." In *Graphics Gems I*, edited by Andrew S. Glassner, pp.144–146, Cambridge, MA: Academic Press, 1990.

[76] Ingmar Peter and Georg Pietrek. "Importance driven construction of photon maps." In *Rendering Techniques '98 (Proceedings of the Ninth Eurographics Workshop on Rendering)*, edited by G. Drettakis and N. Max, pp. 269–280, Vienna: Springer-Verlag, 1998.

[77] M. Pharr and P. Hanrahan. "Monte Carlo evaluation of non-linear scattering equations for subsurface reflection." In *Proceedings of SIGGRAPH 2000, Computer Graphics Proceedings, Annual Conference Series*, edited by Kurt Akeley, pp. 75–84, July 2000.

[78] Bui-T. Phong. "Illumination for computer generated pictures." *Communications of the ACM* 18(6): 311–317 (June 1975).

[79] Pierre Poulin and Alain Fournier. "A model for anisotropic reflection." *Computer Graphics (Proc. SIGGRAPH '90)*, 24(4): 273–282 (August 1990).

[80] Franco P. Preparata and Michael Ian Shamos. *Computational Geometry An Introduction.* New York: Springer-Verlag, 1985.

[81] Reuven Y. Rubinstein. *Simulation and the Monte Carlo Method.* New York: John Wiley & Sons, 1981.

[82] Holly Rushmeier, Charles Patterson, and Aravindan Veerasamy. "Geometric simplification for indirect illumination calculations." In *Proceedings of Graphics Interface '93*, pp. 227–236, Toronto: Canadian Information Processing Society, 1993.

[83] B. Saleh and M. Teich. *Fundamentals of Photonics.* New York: John Wiley & Sons, 1991.

[84] Gernot Schaufler and Henrik Wann Jensen. "Ray tracing point sampled geometry." In *Rendering Techniques 2000*, edited by B. Peroche and H. Rushmeier, pp. 319–328, Vienna: Springer-Verlag, 2000.

[85] Christophe Schlick. "A customizable reflectance model for everyday rendering." In *Fourth Eurographics Workshop on Rendering*, edited by Michael F. Cohen, Claude Puech, and Francois Sillion, pp. 73–84, Eurographics, June 1993.

[86] Robert Sedgewick. *Algorithms in C++.* Reading, MA: Addison-Wesley, 1992.

[87] Peter Shirley. *Physically Based Lighting Calculations for Computer Graphics.* Ph.D. thesis, Dept. of Computer Science, U. of Illinois, Urbana-Champaign, November 1990.

[88] Peter Shirley. "A ray tracing method for illumination calculation in diffuse-specular scenes." In *Proceedings of Graphics Interface '90*, pp. 205–212, Toronto: Canadian Information Processing Society, May 1990.

[89] Peter Shirley. "Discrepancy as a quality measure for sample distributions." In *Eurographics '91*, edited by Werner Purgathofer, pp. 183–194, Amsterdam: North-Holland, September 1991.

[90] Peter Shirley. "Nonuniform random point sets via warping." In *Graphics Gems III*, edited by David Kirk, pp. 80–83, San Diego: Academic Press, 1992.

[91] Peter Shirley. *Realistic ray tracing.* Natick, MA: A K Peters, 2000.

[92] Peter Shirley and Kenneth Chiu. *Notes on adaptive quadrature on the hemisphere.* Technical Report 411, Indiana University, 1995.

[93] Peter Shirley, Bretton Wade, Phillip Hubbard, David Zareski, Bruce Walter, and Donald P. Greenberg. "Global illumination via density estimation." In *Rendering Techniques '95*, edited by P. Hanrahan and W. Purgathofer, pp. 219–230, Vienna: Springer-Verlag, 1995.

[94] Robert Siegel and John R. Howell. *Thermal Radiation Heat Transfer.* Washington, DC: Hemisphere Publishing Corp., 1981.

[95] Francois X. Sillion, James R. Arvo, Stephen H. Westin, and Donald P. Greenberg. "A global illumination solution for general reflectance distributions." *Computer Graphics (Proc. SIGGRAPH '91)* 25(4): 187–196 (July 1991).

[96] B. W. Silverman. *Density Estimation for Statistics and Data Analysis.* Chapman & Hall, 1986.

[97] Jeffrey S. Simonoff. *Smoothing methods in statistics.* New York: Springer-Verlag, 1996.

[98] Brian Smits, James Arvo, and Donald Greenberg. "A clustering algorithm for radiosity in complex environments." In *Proceedings of SIGGRAPH '94, Computer Graphics Proceedings, Annual Conference Series*, edited by Andrew Glassner, pp. 435–442, New York: ACM Press, July 1994.

[99] Brian E. Smits, James R. Arvo, and David H. Salesin. "An importance-driven radiosity algorithm." *Computer Graphics (Proc. SIGGRAPH '92)* 26(2): 273–282 (July 1992).

[100] John M. Snyder and Alan H. Barr. "Ray tracing complex models containing surface tessellations." *Computer Graphics (Proc. SIGGRAPH '87)* 21(4): 119–128 (July 1987).

[101] Jerome Spanier and Ely Gelbard. *Monte Carlo Principles and Neutron Transport Problems.* Reading, MA: Addison-Wesley, 1969.

[102] Jos Stam and Eric Languénou. "Ray tracing in non-constant media." In *Eurographics Rendering Workshop 1996*, edited by Xavier Pueyo and Peter Schröder, pp. 225–234, Vienna: Springer-Verlag.

[103] Marc Stamminger, Philipp Slusallek, and Hans-Peter Seidel. "Three point clustering for radiance computations." In *Rendering Techniques'98*, edited by G. Drettakis and N. Max, pp. 211–222, Vienna: Springer-Verlag, 1998.

[104] Kelvin Sung and Peter Shirley. "Ray tracing with the bsp tree." In *Graphics Gems III*, edited by David Kirk, pp. 271–274, San Diego: Academic Press, 1992.

[105] Frank Suykens and Yves D. Willems. "Density control for photon maps." In *Rendering Techniques 2000*, edited by B. Peroche and H. Rushmeier, pp. 23–34, Vienna: Springer-Verlag, 2000.

[106] K. E. Torrance and E. M. Sparrow. "Theory for off-specular reflection from roughened surfaces." *Journal of Optical Society of America* 57(9): (1967).

[107] Eric Veach. *Robust Monte Carlo methods for light transport simulation.* PhD thesis, Stanford University, 1997.

[108] Eric Veach and Leonidas Guibas. "Bidirectional estimators for light transport." In *Fifth Eurographics Workshop on Rendering*, pp. 147–162, Eurographics, 1994.

[109] Eric Veach and Leonidas J. Guibas. "Optimally combining sampling techniques for Monte Carlo rendering." In *Proceedings of SIGGRAPH 95, Computer Graphics Proceedings, Annual Conference Series*, edited by Robert Cook, pp. 419–428, Reading: MA, Addison Wesley, August 1995.

[110] Eric Veach and Leonidas J. Guibas. "Metropolis light transport." In *Proceedings of SIGGRAPH 97, Computer Graphics Proceedings, Annual Conference Series*, edited by Turner Whitted, pp. 65–76, Reading, MA: Addison Wesley, August 1997.

[111] Vladimir Volevich, Karol Myszkowski, Andrei Khodulev, and Edward A. Kopylov. *Perceptually-informed progressive global illumination solution.* Technical Report 99-1-002, University of Aizu, 1999.

[112] John R. Wallace, Michael F. Cohen, and Donald P. Greenberg. "A two-pass solution to the rendering equation: A synthesis of ray tracing and radiosity methods." *Computer Graphics (Proc. SIGGRAPH '87)* 21(4): pp. 311–320 (July 1987).

[113] Bruce Walter, Philip M. Hubbard, Peter Shirley, and Donald F. Greenberg. "Global illumination using local linear density estimation." *ACM Transactions on Graphics* 16(3): 217–259 (July 1997).

[114] Greg Ward. "Real pixels." In *Graphics Gems II*, edited by James Arvo, pp. 80–83, San Diego: Academic Press, 1991.

[115] Gregory J. Ward. "Measuring and modeling anisotropic reflection." *Computer Graphics (Proc. SIGGRAPH '92)* 26(2): 265–272 (July 1992).

[116] Gregory J. Ward. "The RADIANCE lighting simulation and rendering system." In *Proceedings of SIGGRAPH '94, Computer Graphics Proceedings, Annual Conference Series* edited by Andrew Glassner, pp. 459–472, New York: ACM Press, July 1994.

[117] Gregory J. Ward and Paul Heckbert. "Irradiance gradients." In *Third Eurographics Workshop on Rendering*, pp. 85–98, Eurographics, May 1992.

[118] Gregory J. Ward, Francis M. Rubinstein, and Robert D. Clear. "A ray tracing solution for diffuse interreflection." *Computer Graphics (Proc. SIGGRAPH '88)* 22(4): 85–92 (August 1988).

[119] David Watson and Alistair Mees. "Natural trees—neighbourhood-location in a nut shell." *International Journal of Geographical Information Systems*, 1996.

[120] Turner Whitted. "An improved illumination model for shaded display." *Communications of the ACM* 23(6): 343–349 (June 1980).

[121] Lawrence B. Wolff and David J. Kurlander. "Ray tracing with polarization parameters." *IEEE Computer Graphics and Applications* 10(6): 44–55 (November 1990).

[122] G. Wyszecki and W. S. Stiles. *Color Science: Concepts and Methods, Quantitative Data and Formulae.* New York: John Wiley & Sons, 1982.

[123] Kurt Zimmerman and Peter Shirley. "A two-pass realistic image synthesis method for complex scenes." In *Eurographics Rendering Workshop 1995*, edited by Patrick Hanrahan and Werner Purgathofer, pp. 284–295 Eurographics, June 1995.

Index

Absorption, 18
Absorption coefficient, 114
Adaptive ray marching, 121
Anisotropic reflection, 25
Artistic control, 98, 99

Balanced kd-tree, 70
    Algorithm, 72
Bidirectional path tracing, 43
Blackbody radiation, 17
BRDF, 19
BSSRDF, 18

Caustics photon map, 97
Classic Ray Tracing, 34
Combined estimator, 45
Consistent, 53

Density control, 146
Density estimation, 76, 88
    Nearest neighbor, 78
Depth of field, 38
Diffraction, 12

Diffuse point light, 56
Diffuse reflection, 21, 60
Directional light, 58
Dispersion, 12
Distribution ray tracing, 38

Emitting photons, 55
Extinction coefficient, 114

Finite element techniques, 5
Flux, 14
Form factor, 29
Fresnel equations, 23
Fresnel reflection coefficient, 23

Geometry simplification, 7, 52
Global illumination, 3
Global photon map, 97

Helmholtz law, 20
Henyey-Greenstein phase function, 116
Hybrid techniques, 6

Illuminance, 16
Illumination maps, 52, 75
Importance sampling, 41, 144, 155
Importons, 146
Intensity, 14
Interference, 12
Irradiance, 14
Irradiance caching, 139
Irradiance gradients, 142
Irradiance sampling, 140

Kd-tree, 68
Kernel density estimation, 76

Light intensity, 17
Light transport notation, 30
Local illumination, 18, 20
Low-discrepancy sequence, 147
Luminance, 16
Luminous exitance, 16
Luminous flux, 15
Luminous flux area density, 16
Luminous intensity, 16

Metropolis Light Transport, 47
Microfacets, 25
Monte Carlo integration, 153
Motion blur, 38

Nearest neighbors, 67
Neumann series, 29
Normalized Phong model, 24

Oren-Nayar model, 25

Participating media, 113
    Absorption coefficient, 114
    Anisotropic medium, 116
    Anisotropic scattering, 116
    Isotropic medium, 116
    Isotropic scattering, 116
    Phase function, 115
    Photon tracing, 121
    Radiance estimate, 124
    Ray marching, 119
    Scattering albedo, 123
    Scattering coefficient, 114

    Subsurface scattering, 127
    Volume photon map, 123
    Volume rendering equation, 115
Path integral, 30
Path tracing, 37
Penumbra region, 150
Phase function, 115
    Henyey-Greenstein, 116
    Isotropic scattering, 116
    Mie theory, 118
    Rayleigh, 118
    Schlick, 117
Phong model, 24
Photometry, 15
Photon, 13
Photon emission, 55
Photon gathering, 83
Photon map, 54
    Balanced kd-tree, 70
    Balancing algorithm, 71
    Data structure, 67
    Kd-tree, 70
    Locating photons, 72
    Memory layout, 71
    Photon structure, 69
    Radiance estimate, 78
Photon mapping, 54
Photon optics, 12
Photon scattering, 60
Photon structure, 69
Photon tracing, 54
Physically-based simulation, 3
Planck's formula, 17
Point light, 56
Point light source, 36
Polarization, 12
Power heuristic, 45
Primary rays, 35
Projection map, 59, 98

QMC, 147
Quasi-Monte Carlo, 147

Radiance, 14
Radiance estimate, 78
    Pseudocode, 81

Radiant energy, 13
Radiant exitance, 14
Radiant flux, 14
Radiant intensity, 14
Radiometry, 13
Radiosity, 5, 14, 29
Radiosity equation, 29
Ray marching, 119
Ray optics, 12
Ray tracing, 34
    Algorithm, 36
Realistic image synthesis, 2
Reciprocity, 20
Recursive ray marching, 121
Recursive ray tracing, 34
Reflectance, 20
Reflection, 60
Reflection models, 24
Refraction, 23
Rendering equation, 27
Russian roulette, 61, 123

Scattering coefficient, 114
Schlick's Reflection Model, 25, 61
Shadow photons, 101, 148

Shadow ray, 36
Snell's law, 23
Specular reflection, 22, 60
Specular refraction, 23
Spherical light, 57
Square light, 58
Stochastic sampling, 38
Stratified sampling, 41, 155
Subsurface scattering, 19, 127

Tone mapping, 16
Torrance-Sparrow model, 24

Unbiased, 34, 53

Variance reduction, 41
Visibility function, 28
Visual importance, 145
Volume photon map, 123
Volume radiance estimate, 124
Voronoi diagram, 69

Wattage, 17
Wave optics, 12
Wavelength, 18

Plate I. Path tracing can simulate full global illumination, but often results in noisy images as seen in this simple box scene. (See Figure 3.5)

Plate II. Finite element radiosity algorithms are good at simulating diffuse interreflection as seen in this replica of the widely used Cornellbox. (See Figure 1.4)

Plate III. Photon mapping can simulate full global illumination in complex models as seen in this rendering of an architectural model. (See Figure 1.2)

Plate IV. A caustic through a glass of cognac. (See Figure 8.9)

Plate V. A close-up of the caustic in Plate IV. (See Figure 8.10)

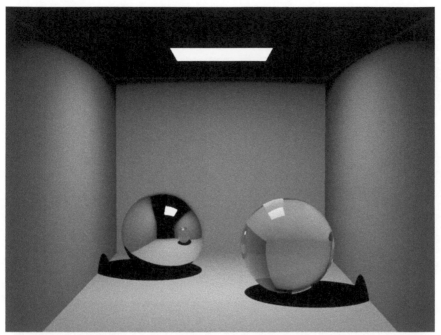

Plate VI. The box scene ray-traced. (See Figure 9.10)

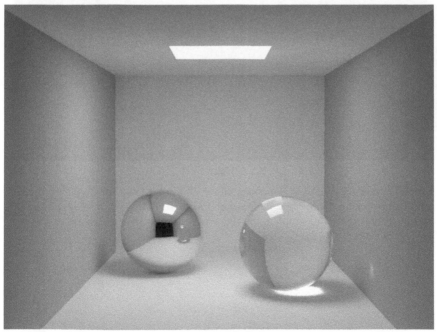

Plate VII. The box scene with full global illumination. (See Figure 9.9)

12:30pm

6:30pm

Plate VIII. A rendering of a geometric model of Little Matterhorn with trees (200 million polygon) in the middle of the day and at sunset. We used just 100,000 photons for this model to simulate the illumination from the sun as well as the sky. (See Figure 9.16)

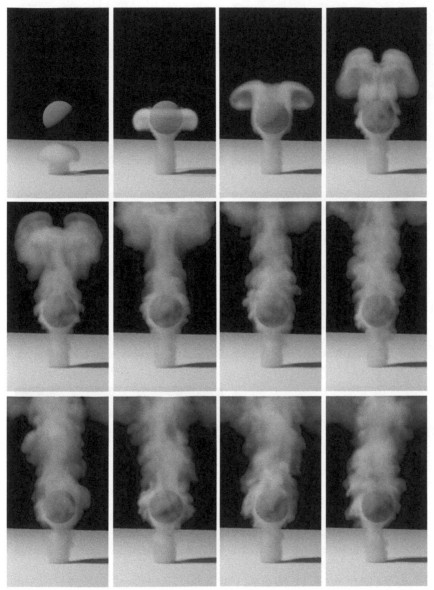

Plate IX. Sequence of rendered images from a simulation of smoke flowing past a sphere (from [25]). (See Figure 10.11)

7am

8am

10am

3pm

6pm

7pm

Plate X. A simulation of the lighting in the unbuilt "Courtyard House with Curved Elements" by Ludwig Mies van der Rohe. (See Figure 9.17)

(a)   (b)

(c)   (d)

Plate XI. A weathering simulation of a granite sphinx from [23]. (a) is the fresh granite, (b) shows erosion due to salt, (c) shows reddening due to dissolved iron, and (d) shows the combined weathering effect due to salt and iron. (See Figure 10.14)

Plate XII. A translucent marble bust. (See Figure 10.16)

Plate XIII. A diffuse rendering of the marble bust. (See Figure 10.17)